Bare Your Soul

. . . The moment when both crown chakras merge, you will feel ignited with awesome force. As both of your beings unite in a solitary, blazing fire of energy, darts of light will spark away from you. For the first few moments, you will feel power surge through you with pleasure beyond comprehension, and then all within a breath, you will find that your consciousness is completely drawn inward. When this drawing in occurs, you momentarily become unaware of your partner, your own thoughts, your own ecstasy . . .

Naked Soul removes the mystery, illusion, and misinterpretation of the very real and ancient art of lovemaking in the spirit realm:

- Learn several tried-and-true techniques for astral projection and find the one that works best for you
- Contact a soul guide to lead you through the astral planes
- Find an astral lover as well as the ultimate spiritual cosmic mate
- Learn to practice and understand astral love
- Discover how to have soul sex while still in the physical body
- Unite with other soul energies through the six types of spirit melding
- Gain insight into same-sex relationships, both in the physical and spirit realms
- Protect yourself from lower-level entities

. . . Suddenly you will only be. This loss of identity and awareness of time and matter will usher you into a state of bliss that you have never experienced in your physical body. You will feel completely inseparable from all of creation . . .

About the Author

Marlené Marie Druhan is a conscious medium, visionary/aura artist, fine portrait artist, instrumental composer, and instructor. Raised in the lush beauty of rural Pennsylvania and New Jersey, her medium-istic abilities were nurtured in a metaphysical home. Beginning her out-of-body travels at age fifteen, Marlené has traveled extensively within the finer realms of existence, bringing these wonderful and beautiful experiences into her writing and paintings. Through her soul travel ability, she has gained much knowledge of cosmic rela-tionships, inner plane healing, and the secrets of traveling in the soul body with intention, ease, and success.

Marlené has coordinated workshops such as *Dancing with the Goddess: Women's Spirituality, Movement Meditation, and Elemental Identity; Art as a Spiritual Link;* and *A Place to Be Me! Classes for the Creative Child.* Her goal is to be a part of a new Golden Age of the arts and spiritual sciences that she hopes to see in her lifetime.

To Write to the Author

If you wish to contact the author or would like more information about this book, please write to the author in care of Llewellyn Worldwide and we will forward your request. Both the author and publisher appreciate hearing from you and learning of your enjoy-ment of this book and how it has helped you. Llewellyn Worldwide cannot guarantee that every letter written to the author can be answered, but all will be forwarded. Please write to:

Marlené Marie Druhan
℅ Llewellyn Worldwide
P.O. Box 64383, Dept. K247-X
St. Paul, MN 55164-0383, U.S.A.

Please enclose a self-addressed stamped envelope for reply, or $1.00 to cover costs.
If outside U.S.A., enclose international postal reply coupon.

Marlené Marie Druhan

Naked Soul

Astral

Travel

& Cosmic

Relationships

1998
Llewellyn Publications
St. Paul, Minnesota 55164-0383 U.S.A.

FIRST EDITION
First Printing, 1998

Cover art from Digital Stock Photography
Cover design by Lisa Novak
Editing and book design by Rebecca Zins
Illustration on page 10 by Carrie Westfall

Library of Congress Cataloging-in-Publication Data
Druhan, Marlené Marie, 1969–
Naked soul: astral travel & cosmic relationships /
Marlené Marie Druhan.—1st ed.
p. cm.
Includes bibliographical references and index.
ISBN 1-56718-247-X (pbk.)
1. Astral projection.   2. Guides (Spiritualism)
3. Love—Miscellanea.   I. Title.
BF1389.A7D78   1998
133.9'5—dc21
98-30546
CIP

Publisher's Note: Llewellyn Worldwide does not participate in, endorse,
or have any authority or responsibility concerning private business
transactions between our authors and the public.
All mail addressed to the author is forwarded but the
publisher cannot, unless specifically instructed by the author,
give out an address or phone number.

Printed in the U.S.A.

Llewellyn Publications
A Division of Llewellyn Worldwide, Ltd.
P.O. Box 64383, Dept. 247-X
St. Paul, MN 55164-0383, U.S.A.

Dedication

To Winifred M. Druhan, mother, teacher, friend,
Madonna of my heart . . . thank you for teaching me
the greatest lesson of all: nothing is impossible.
You are the most beautiful soul in God's gallery.

And to my father, Thomas L. Druhan,
the brightest star in heaven . . . thank you
for molding the clay of my youth and for your quiet wisdom.
Thank you both for all of your countless sacrifices.
My greatest accomplishment is being your daughter
and always will be.
I love you!

My spirit breaks the bonds of flesh

And soars the heavens high

And sees a world no mortal sees

When I behold my Beloved's eyes.

Winifred M. Druhan

Contents

Contents

Acknowledgments

To Pamela Frieda Fleming, soul sister and confidant, for your wild and beautiful spirit and for being an oasis when my life is a desert.

To my family . . . Helen E. Crowther, aunt and unforgettable woman, for her enthusiasm and support through the years. To Allen Troyano, uncle and guardian angel, for his generous heart and humor. To Frieda A. Currin, my "Aunt-Tot", for being living proof that miracles exist and for her intrepid spirit. And to a star that burned out too soon, Robert Brian Currin, cousin and great thinker; thank you for passing this way on your journey home. We mourn your absence, but rejoice because you've only just begun. I love all of you more than you know!

To Sanschi, my eternal heart, "Hyun lean dram, wa Sodima . . . ."

Acknowledgments

To my muse, my "Somewhere in Time," husband of my soul . . . thank you for your brilliance, the sustenance of your love, and the ecstasy of your existence. You are my completion and fire in the night. I love you and will dance with you forever.

To James DeBiasio and Colin Marshall, mystics and beacons of my childhood . . . thank you for your spiritual gifts.

To Michelle St. Andre . . . thank you for being an angel during difficult times.

To Eddie, who carried me over turbulent waters many a night, many a lifetime. Thank you forevermore.

To Carl Weschcke and Llewellyn Worldwide for harvesting my words.

To my Guardians Judy, Lani, Lightning Hawk, Mari, Yeshua, Lord Ganesha, Father God and Mother Goddess, and to all of the Helping Spirits for guiding me and blessing me. This is for you.

And lastly, to my little familiar and truest friend, my four-legged angel, Simon Peter, who will always be mine.

Introduction

The *American Heritage* dictionary on my desk defines the word *soul* as "the animating and vital principle often conceived as an immaterial entity that survives death." If we look at this definition through purely intellectual eyes, we are given the impression that the soul is unseen, unheard, and unfelt—therefore, in the category of all fanciful facts that can only be useful to poets and visionaries. Yet even before there was what we could call language, there was a universal belief in the human soul. There is not a single known religion, ancient or modern, that does not take into account this very essence of an individual. For something that cannot be perceived with the five physical senses, it certainly has been an unavoidable object of wonder, religious debate, and hope since time began. As invisible and vital as the air we breathe, the soul, by definition, gives life to the flesh.

Throughout the ancient world, the soul received as much attention, validation, and reverence as the body itself. In our modern world, the soul is often seen as no more than poetic theory; yet those who have experienced enlightenment, trauma, illness, or who have come back from clinical death, describe what it is like to be in the soul body, separated from the physical body. Many describe the out-of-body experience as a journey to other realms of existence—an afterlife that waits beyond our physical world.

Ancient cultures not only believed in this human soul and its capabilities but also in the souls of animals, plants, trees, elements, and minerals. The ancient Greeks honored the soul of every living thing. The spirit of the smallest pebble to the most majestic of mountains was accounted for in daily life as well as in ritual customs and sacred festivals. The Greeks' timeless mythology is brightly colored with spirits, gods, goddesses, demigods, and fantastic creatures. The physical world and spirit realms were intricately interwoven and never divided.

Ancient Egyptians portrayed the life and activities of the *ba,* or soul, on the walls of their temples and tombs. As part of their spiritual belief system, ancient Egyptians supposed that each man and woman not only had one soul, but seven.

Most ancient cultures' words for the soul were feminine. Many believed that every person, whether male or female, had a feminine soul essence inherited from the Great Mother Goddess through the physical birth mother. Vedic India, on the other hand, believed that a person's primary soul was derived from the male–father principle, while lesser soul qualities, including name, heart, and mind, were inherited from the mother. Due to this theory it was customary for Brahman fathers to breathe upon a newborn three times to deposit the soul into the infant's body.

Cultures varied in their beliefs of where the soul actually resided within the physical body. Many thought its dwelling place was in the liver area, while others believed it to dwell within the heart. Patriarchal believers claimed that the souls of all offspring existed solely in the testicles.

Astral projection, the separation of soul or consciousness from the physical body, was perhaps most validated and valued by tribal cultures. The shaman, or medicine man, ingested peyote and other hallucinogens prior to a ceremony to prompt the spirit from the body during trance states. Through projection of soul and consciousness, the shaman interacted with spirits and brought healing back to the tribe.

The ancient Chinese achieved astral projection through deep meditation. Eastern seekers accomplished it through the path and practice of yoga, but were discouraged because astral projection was (and is) considered to be one of many *siddhis,* or obstacles to true and total enlightenment. Other siddhis include all psychic, paranormal, and supernatural phenomena. The Sufis, Islamic mystics, induced consciousness expansion and ecstatic states with dancing, spinning, and writing sacred poetry. Medieval Witches or Wiccans prepared flying ointments composed of mystical, hallucinogenic, and often toxic herbs that were rubbed into the skin to provoke or simulate astral projection.

Though the projected human soul is most often invisible to the physical eye, it is sometimes seen by the living as if it is the actual physical person. The human double or specter of a living person that is seen still lingers in our cultural language in terms such as the German *doppelgängar* ("double walker"), the English/Irish *fetch,* and the Swedish *vardoger.* Within superstitious and occult beliefs, seeing someone's double is a portent of the seer's own death. English poet Percy Bysshe Shelley saw his own double not long before his tragic drowning at age thirty.

Many agree that the soul's history and its projected state are interesting, but question the purpose of leaving the body at will. Is it allowed in the religious scheme of things? Shouldn't the soul's exit from the body be reserved only for natural death? Isn't it just the glamour of the devil enticing individuals with power? The answer to all of these questions is multidimensional. Why do we pray? We pray to build a link between ourselves and Deity. The same for astral projection. Why do we meditate, contemplate, visualize, or study religion and spirituality? We do these things to better understand our true selves and to lead happier, more meaningful lives. The same for astral projection. Why do we seek knowledge of science, medicine, astronomy, or physics? We strive to learn these subjects to discover and comprehend the unknown. The same for astral projection. In short, astral projection is a tool to unearth the greater, unknown portion of ourselves and all that exists. Is it a power snag on the way to enlightenment? Yes, if a person only pursues the art to have egotistic or psychic power over others. Is it okay to experiment, to see what happens? Yes, provided the person knows the facts and the possible dangers of occult curiosity. Is it used as an escape from "real" life? Yes, provided the person forgets that the physical body and physical life are unavoidable and necessary for fulfilling his or her purpose on this planet at this time.

Astral projection and soul travel are as natural to our spiritual selves as breathing is to our physical selves. Contrary to common belief and fear, astral projection is not a by-product or symptom of mental illness, hallucination, or satanic practice nor is it only reserved for ecstatic saints or very enlightened masters. Death does not have to occur in order to have access to invisible realms of being, those inner planes of existence commonly called astral planes. Soul travelers know that "dying" is a spiritual art that can be learned while living. Projection of the soul, most often associated with death, need not be an inevitable fear; it may instead be cultivated as a sacred practice for spiritual growth.

No matter who you are, where you live, how old or young you are, which lifestyle you choose, or which religion you practice, you are already a soul traveler. You share a common experience with all human beings: astral projection during sleep, whether you remember your journeys or not. Those who experience, without trauma, unplanned projection during waking hours most often leave the body during meditation, lovemaking (at or near the moment of orgasm), the twilight state of relaxation just prior to sleep, or through the use of recreational drugs. *Naked Soul* is intended for those who wish to learn the art of leaving the body at will without undergoing extreme conditions or drug use. Soul travel is a beautiful but practical craft anyone can learn with patience, determination, faith, and a sincere heart. After time, practice, and errors, I learned to travel in the soul body fully conscious, acute, confident, and at any time I wished to. *Naked Soul* is the harvest of thirteen years of soul travel experience. It does not introduce soul travel, but its goal is to present the lifestyle of soul travel.

No matter if you tried to astral project a million times and have not succeeded or if you already are a soul traveler, I invite you along on the journey of this book. You will find several unique, tried and true techniques of projection, an in-depth discussion on soul guides and how to soul travel with them, detailed information on the nature and ability of the soul body, and vivid first-person accounts of breathtaking inner planes and how to get there. *Naked Soul* also focuses on spirit lovers, lovemaking, and melding (exchanging and fusing of soul energies) in the soul body for spiritual ecstasy, healing, and transformation for both the heterosexual and same-sex couple. If you have loved ones beyond death's threshold and you wish to continue a loving, constant relationship with them, *Naked Soul* also takes the soul traveler into the afterlife and the immense possibilities of non-romantic relationships.

In our present age of violence, greed, AIDS, and emotionally bankrupt relationships, we must again discover the original innocence of our spiritual and erotic selves. As soul travelers, we are able to remember our true, original selves. We all had a soul before we had a body. Traveling in this soul body brings us again to a state of pristine consciousness that we can take back to our physical bodies and our daily lives. By doing this, we reclaim the true sustenance of living.

So, as you embark on your own spiritual journeys, remember that your soul is unique and so will be your experiences. May you make beautiful discoveries!

Part One

The Soul Traveler as Explorer

Chapter One

Looking Skyward

Preparation

and Protection

Raised in a metaphysical family, I took it for granted that my father practiced mind power and my mother was a soul traveler. It didn't confuse me that my childhood peers did not meditate with their parents or look for nature spirits in fragrant October forests. Reared in this protective bubble of alternative spirituality that embraced all

Who is the intrepid Seeker
Who plunges into the abyss like a sword
To pierce the black vision
To find an angel singing?

religions, I learned to accept the differences of others as well as how to cope being from a different kind of family. What *did* bother me was my inability to follow in my mother's footsteps. She often spoke about her exhilarating journeys out of body to European cathedrals where she touched glowing angels painted on Gothic domes and tasted succulent fruit from glimmering orchards not of this world. Throughout my childhood and early teens, I struggled to astral project. I did deep breathing, yoga, meditation, and visualization, to no avail. The harder I tried, the more grounded I became. I abandoned my quest. During this period of non-activity I found myself becoming open to the spirit world, which eventually enabled me to realize my life-long goal. A year and a half after giving up on astral projection, gradually, effortlessly, I found myself out of my body. Despite my upbringing, I was shocked but thrilled to find my own spiritual abilities and, looking back now, I was also unprepared. In the course of years to follow, I learned painfully how important it is to shield oneself from negative people and situations if spiritual advancement without consequences is to be achieved. This is why I ask you, the reader, to take some time to go through the simple preparations in this chapter before embarking on the soul travel quest. Equally preparing the body, mind, and spirit ensures quicker results, reliable protection, and spiritual balance.

Don't worry if you feel overwhelmed or cannot memorize all the information you need in this chapter. This chapter is the collective knowledge I've gained over the past thirteen years that you may benefit from and is here if and when the need arises. For now, take what you need and look forward to your journeys in the spirit body.

Preparation

If we are to maintain peak performance and prevent injury, we prepare our bodies before physical activity; the same should be considered before we look skyward. If you haven't yet experienced astral projection or if you do on a regular basis, take a few days or weeks to focus on each: body, mind, and spirit.

As you read the following pages of preparation, you will find that each category will overlap with the others. It is impossible to separate the body from the mind, the mind from the spirit, and so forth. So, if one of our three selves is developed and prepared more so than the others, it will pose a problem somewhere in the course of your spiritual progress.

Preparation of the Physical Body and Physical Life

The physical body is the temple of our souls and the vehicle we use to experience earthly life. It is the nucleus of our greatest human joy as well as our pain. If the body is unhealthy, so will be our spiritual selves. From my own experience, having good health is the most important asset a soul traveler can have. Pain, fatigue, stress, and intoxification all have a negative influence on soul travel, at times even hindering it. Getting enough sleep; eating whole, non-processed foods; and moving the body in exercise ensures a positive foundation for our greatest health potential.

Having a healthy body also means having a healthy aura. The aura is the etheric, protective shield that surrounds the body. In a healthy state, this multicolored, flame-like force field acts as a psychic moat, obstructing negative or harmful energies from entering our spiritual space. Poor health, addiction, negative emotion, negative people or situations, and poor diet all weaken this beautiful spiritual shield. When the aura is weakened, it loses its inborn power to give us psychic protection and allows harmful entities and energies into our physical, mental and spiritual space. The most significant enemy to a healthy aura is a weak, tired, or sick physical body.

As physical preparation for soul travel, strive daily to eat only high-vibrational foods that still have the life force intact. These foods are whole, unprocessed grains and fresh vegetables and fruit (preferably organic), fresh juices, herbal decaffeinated beverages, and foods that don't have processed sugars, preservatives, and artificial additives. It is unnecessary to be vegan or vegetarian as long as your meat intake is balanced with plenty of the aforementioned foods. If you feel an affinity to plant energies, you may wish to drink teas made from herbs that have a long mystical tradition. Yarrow flowers, mugwort, peppermint, rosemary, and lemongrass have long been used by mystics to stimulate the psychic centers. From experience, these herbs work best alone. They can be purchased at health food stores or herbal suppliers and are completely safe, non-habit forming, caffeine free, and produce results when taken faithfully.

Preparing the body for soul travel through positive eating habits is enhanced by some form of creative or spiritually based movement. Tai Chi, yoga, easy stretching, walking, ballet, and ethnic or ritual dance are all wonderful forms of exercise that work with the body's natural rhythms and encourage creativity. Even if you have a firm exercise schedule that includes sports and workouts, these gentle movements are wonderful additions to your routine. Perhaps before that five-mile run or one-hour aerobics class you can choose yoga or Tai Chi to loosen up your muscles and soothe your soul. Proper exercise and creative movements in any form stimulate etheric and psychic energies that can become dormant when the body is idle too long.

A weekly psychically cleansing bath also prepares the body for projection. Once a week, add the following to your bath water:

Cleansing Bath

¼ cup pure sea salt or 1 cup ocean water
3 capfuls pure rose water
5 drops pure essential oil of myrrh, jasmine, or sandalwood

If you shower, simply dissolve one tablespoon of pure sea salt with three capfuls of pure rosewater and three drops of pure essential oil of myrrh, jasmine, or sandalwood in two cups of water from your shower and pour over your body after cleansing. Whether you bathe or shower, do not rinse the fragranced salt water off. As you bathe or shower, imagine the week's negativity washing down the drain, leaving your body and aura shimmering clean. Water not only cleanses you physically but also astrally, as does pure sea salt. Rosewater, myrrh, jasmine, and sandalwood are all high-vibrational fragrances that stimulate spiritual awareness.

Your physical surroundings are also very important to your soul travel and spiritual success. Keep your environment physically clean from dirt and clutter. A cluttered room interferes with positive energy waves that are conducive to psychic and spiritual work. To keep your environment psychically charged with good energy, play beautiful, uplifting music that makes you feel joyful, creative, loving, or spiritual. Fragrance also channels higher energy, and you may wish to burn incense or use natural potpourris or misters. Choose products that are made from only pure essential oils and fragrances, not artificial or semi-pure substances, as artificial fragrance is spiritually worthless. Again, if you have an affinity to plant energies, you may wish to fill small bowls with mystical herbs and put them by your bed or near any other place you plan on doing your spiritual or soul travel work. Mugwort, poplar leaves, or rosemary all have magical history in promoting astral projection when placed near the physical body. If you have an affinity to minerals, stones, and gems, you may also add these to your herb bowls. Hematite, celestite, and amethyst are said to encourage astral projection. You may even wish to wear them as jewelry.

Lastly, but most importantly, I would like to discourage the use of any recreational drugs—including alcohol—in spiritual and psychic activity. LSD, marijuana, mescaline, heroin, mushrooms, and alcohol all weaken the aura despite positive experiences that many have had while under their influence. These mind-altering substances may open an individual to the mystical but they also unavoidably leave an individual vulnerable to negative forces. Many of you may dispute this fact because of the history of hallucinogens in the tribal shaman's* life. What must be considered here is the thorough training a shaman undergoes. This life-long vocation is based on many years of arduous study of the mystical arts with an elder, either living or in the spirit world. No matter how dedicated we are to our spiritual training and evolvement, our lives differ from that of the shaman's because most of us must deal with the outside world constantly. This means we are always surrounded by the negativities of society and we are forever in the process of shielding the purity of our spiritual quests from these influences. The shaman, on the other hand, is constantly surrounded by like-minded people who encourage, support, revere, and nurture his vocation and special abilities. Over a period of many challenging years, the shaman learns his trade, so to speak, and is prepared to use hallucinogens as a sacred practice. Since we work and raise families in our modern world, I believe that very few of us can live a sheltered shaman's life, no matter how we try or think we are succeeding. We may try recreational drugs in a very inspired moment and have a beautiful and shimmering mystical experience but, after these first few times, the drugs begin to puncture that taut psychic resistance of the aura until it becomes so slack that negative forces flow into our space with unchallenged ease. Our drug use, no matter how ceremonial, does not contain the preparation, positive environment, and spiritual power of the shaman's drug use.

Most importantly, the shaman is trained to leave his body both without the use of drugs as well as with the aid of artificial stimulants. When we use drugs to aid our mystical experience, we become

* A shaman can be either male or female, but for easier reading and continuity, I chose to refer to the male practitioner. Male and female shamans possess equal power.

8

accustomed to relying on the substances and not our own inborn shamanic gifts.

Drug use is a direct solicitation for dark energies that wait patiently until they find a gateway into a spiritual seeker's life. These gateways are the holes and gaps in an unhealthy aura. So I advise that you seek to discover and polish your natural mystical ability; this way you are preserving the light and strength of your aura while being spiritually independent. How to protect your physical and spirit body, how to avoid occult dangers, and common fears will all be addressed under the "Protection" section later in this chapter.

Preparation of the Mind and Emotional Life

If our physical bodies and surroundings are correctly balanced and prepared for soul travel but our emotions are not, then there is still a risk of energy loss and aura impairment. The emotions of the soul traveler are equally important for positive and successful journeys.

The emotions are directly related to the etheric power centers of the body, known as chakras. The word *chakra* means "wheel" in Sanskrit because of the swirling light energy of these spiritual centers that are located along the length of the spine.

Traditionally there are seven major chakras, beginning at the base of the spine and concluding at the top of the head. Each chakra corresponds to a different organ function in the physical body, responds to particular types of emotion, exudes and vibrates at a particular color, and possesses its own unique sound. The Kundalini, the Sanskrit word for the inherent spiritual force or serpent fire, sleeps at the base of the spine until activated. The goal of many Eastern religions is to awaken this mystical power that, only when it is awakened, travels upward through each chakra until it reaches the crown chakra at the top of the head. Once the Kundalini reaches this highest chakra center, the individual reaches a state of enlightenment or cosmic consciousness.

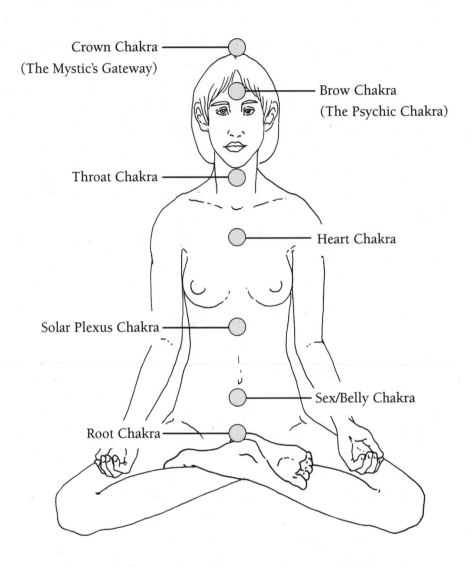

Crown Chakra
(The Mystic's Gateway)

Brow Chakra
(The Psychic Chakra)

Throat Chakra

Heart Chakra

Solar Plexus Chakra

Sex/Belly Chakra

Root Chakra

Major Chakras of the Physical and Spiritual Bodies

Unreleased anger, frustration, grief, sexual energy, and unresolved fear become lodged in the chakras, making it very difficult if not impossible for the Kundalini power to travel upward. Once a chakra becomes littered with the etheric energies of unresolved or unexpressed emotions, the chakra becomes sluggish, its good energy corked, and eventually it is unable to function. Therefore, I cannot stress enough the importance of releasing anger when it is felt (within reason and without harm to another person), grief when it is welling up inside, and sexual energy before it becomes frustration. If each of us would deal with the emotion and situation at hand, there would be no accumulation of unwanted, worthless energy in the chakras and most of us would probably experience our spiritual and creative potential much sooner.

With the insistence of one of my soul guides, over a two-week period I dealt with the emotions at hand, cried when I felt like crying, screamed when I felt like screaming, and so on. I was amazed to realize what I had buried, trying to stay "strong" without releasing feelings. The first few days were almost unbearable in intensity but, after seeing the first week through, I felt lighter than I had in years. It was as though I had emerged from a dark tomb and saw the sunlight. When the two-week period reached its end, I found myself on fire with creativity and joy just to be alive. Most of all, I was traveling in the soul body like never before. The effortless, ecstatic journeys of that time were possible by my willingness to be vulnerable enough to feel and then let it go.

We are all encouraged by society from a very early age to be in control, strong, and impervious to deep emotion. As a result, as adults we find ourselves numb to joy, embittered by experience, unable to love with our whole selves, and sexually inhibited or promiscuous, unable or fearful to commit to one person. In reality, we are our strongest when we have the courage to fully feel. As part of your emotional and mental preparation for soul travel, take a few days or weeks (the longer the better) to allow emotions to surface. If you are thinking right now, *If I cry, I'll never stop,* then you are in more need of emotional release than you realize and probably have years of unreleased feelings trapped in your chakras and even in the cells of your physical body. Dare to feel, to enter that dark room we fill with anger and uncried tears and then throw open the curtains and let in the light of peace and forgiveness. It may be a long road, but it is well worth the effort. Once I did this in my own life, I progressed at lightning speed in my own spiritual pursuits and even experienced physical healing.

So, while you are preparing physically, prepare emotionally and give your heart a well-deserved and long-awaited house cleaning. But remember that once is not enough. Keeping the chakras clean takes maintenance and means that it is a moment-to-moment dedication. During the times I don't release emotion, giving it license to fester and take hold of my well-being with parasitic tenacity, my spiritual abilities lose power and my physical energy dwindles to a flicker. So, even though it is difficult, sometimes inconvenient, and even frightening, the results are worth all of it.

To prepare mentally for soul travel, take a few moments a day to plan where you will go once you leave your body. Write down all the places, as if you are planning a wonderful trip. Read about your earthly destinations and dream about the ones you will discover within the inner planes. While you do this, ask yourself why you want to travel in the soul body. Your answers may be something like this: To visit Aunt Mary who died last year; to see beautiful celestial cities; et cetera. If you find your answers involve spying on your ex-lover or that gorgeous person who works at the bookstore or being the first one in your meditation group to do it, then take a minute (and be honest) to remember what truly gives you fulfillment. Yes, we are all human and have human moments when we have burning desires to haunt or seek mischievous revenge or see if that celebrity really is a good lover, but as soul travelers and spiritual seekers, we must follow a reasonable code of ethics. To reach our mystical potential, following the Golden Rule should be our first goal: Do unto others only what you would have done unto you. For greatest success, we should strive to adhere to the following:

- Allow others their physical, emotional, and spiritual space, including privacy

- Remember there is a fine line between the Black Arts (occult practices that involve manipulation, revenge, psychic infliction) and the Spiritual Arts (mystical and positive occult practices that aim for the highest good for all concerned); live and astral project by the above-mentioned Golden Rule

- Feed the soul, not the lower self or ego; strive for spiritual/psychic/mystical progress to reach fullest potential, not to have power over others, appear holier, or use spiritual abilities as a badge of pride

Lastly, as mental and emotional preparation, study the chakra chart if you are unfamiliar with the chakras or need to brush up (page 10). Techniques for projection found in this book involve these spiritual centers. But most importantly, sing, dance, play with animals and children, paint, love and be loved; joy is the most valuable emotional asset a soul traveler can have. When we take time to be free, we find happiness, and when we are happy, we can accomplish great things.

Preparation of the Spirit and Psychic Life

Once the physical body is prepared, the emotions and mind are at peace, and then spiritual preparation is possible. If the body or emotions are not prepared equally, spiritual and psychic preparation will be very difficult.

Spiritual preparation for soul travel means making time to do spiritually minded activities. Reading spiritual or sacred books, meditating, praying, visiting a house of worship, or making your own special altar to do your spiritual work are activities that direct your consciousness away from the mundane so that mystical experience can happen. Even if it means taking the phone off the hook, dropping the kids off at a friend's house, or missing that favorite television show, making time for spiritual work is the most important thing we can do. We do physical workouts to get the body in its healthiest and most attractive form, and the same should be done for our spirits. Soul workouts lift us from the chains of daily obligation, frustration, and mundane concerns and give our souls a place to dance and be what they inherently are—free.

Due to the balancing act many of us perform with career and family life, it is difficult to reserve time and space so our souls receive the attention they need. To stay connected to the heavenly mainland in stormy physical seas, we must take a few moments each day to read a page or two of a spiritual book, pray, meditate, spend contemplative time in nature, or simply acknowledge a Higher Power when we see something beautiful. Doing these small things is the most lucrative investment we can make. In the long run, through finding inner harmony, we become better parents, workers, friends, and lovers.

During the days and weeks you find time for spiritual activity, try to avoid books and movies that focus on negative occultism, as well as psychic tools that can invite unwanted entities, such as the Ouija board. Save the séances and horror for another time, if at all.

As psychic preparation, imagine throughout the day that your entire body is encased in a protective bubble of white fire. Imagine that each ray of this psychic light has a spear-tipped edge pointing away from you, serving as etheric armor. If you are in the company of a draining person, it is especially good to practice this visualization. This simple psychic exercise increases the strength and protective power of your natural aura and is a preliminary to the techniques of protection that will be discussed later in this chapter.

Spiritual and psychic preparation should include anything that makes you feel connected to a Higher Power, so feel free to choose your own spiritual inspiration.

Preparation on the Day of Soul Travel Attempt

The best time to attempt any of the projection techniques presented in this book in between meals, when you are neither hungry nor too full. This means that if you have a chattering stomach or a very satisfied one, projection will be difficult. From my own experience, projection right after meals invites failure, for while the body is still in the early stages of digestion, the spirit body is too grounded in the physical to release. On the other hand, being hungry is too much of a distraction, and any distraction from the desired goal grounds the spirit. Many people, including shamans, fast before attempting to leave the body, but again, from experience, I do not advocate it. During a fast, the body's blood sugar levels can fluctuate. When the blood sugar lowers, there is a loss of vitality and energy in the physical body that can have a weakening effect on the aura, thus giving lower energies and entities a chance to enter your psychic/astral space. Choose a time when you feel comfortable between meals.

I've experienced nearly effortless projections and long journeys when I attempted soul travel immediately after exercising. Even from a simple but stimulating walk, the circulation is more active and oxygen intake reaches the brain. Oxygen intake is essential for psychic and spiritual work because when we take in oxygen, it reaches not only the physical organs and cells of the body but also the psychic centers or chakras. When organs are stimulated, chakras are also more active. The psychic energy of the body begins to move when the blood moves, so a good walk or workout can increase your chances of soul travel success.

The place you choose to attempt projection is very important. The environment and time of day that enable you to reach a state of relaxation in order to leave the body should be chosen carefully. A quiet, darkened room has worked best for me, yet sitting or reclining comfortably indoors in a pathway of sunlight has also enabled me to experience positive and successful journeys. When you choose your space, be sure you will be undisturbed and that people, pets, phones, televisions, radios, and clocks are not distracting you. If you can catch that moment when there is as little noise as possible, by all means, attempt projection then. If you choose an outdoor space, be sure you are completely safe and undisturbed by strangers, insects, and temperature changes.

The physical body should not be too warm or too cool but covered with a sheet or light blanket, for body temperature tends to lower during projection. Many times I've left my body in a perfectly comfortable state and, on returning, found myself to be very cold. If you wish, you can attempt projection skyclad (in the nude). Freedom from clothing can have a profound effect on projection. Our psychic or spiritual energy is often stronger when there is an absence of clothing because clothes can hold mundane or negative energy that is collected during daily living. Being nude has a positive effect also because it is a pure state—the state in which we came into the world.

Early morning, twilight, and night hours are best for soul travel. At these times, noise is less and the energies of the mundane physical world are less active and intrusive.

Most importantly, never attempt projection or practice soul travel when you are tired, emotionally charged (negatively), ill, intoxicated, seriously depressed, intensely sexually frustrated, or in the company of anyone with an active addiction. All of these states create entrances for lower energies and invite negative experiences. Always take precaution and use a protection technique before each attempt at projection or soul travel.

Protection

Most soul travelers experience positive journeys and projections most of the time, but there are times when a negative journey breaks the nearly perfect record of wonderful experiences of even the most seasoned soul traveler. Knowing how to avoid negative situations and having awareness of the possible dangers of soul travel is necessary, much like wearing a life jacket when we spend a day on the water. Chances are slim that we will ever need the life jacket but, if and when we do need it, it will be there. The same for knowing protection techniques and knowing the few but very real psychic dangers of travelling in the spirit body.

During the thirteen years of experiencing planned, conscious out-of-body journeys, I can count on my hand the number of unpleasant ones. These were minor annoyances involving problems with grounding or mischievous but harmless spirits. But there was one incident when I found myself unprepared and very vulnerable despite a solid foundation of experience.

Possession is a controversial subject but one that must be examined in relation to the art of soul travel. The incident that happened to me, I believe, was what could be defined as a possession attempt. It was during a very difficult period of health problems, when my body and mind were very weary. Though I was not out of body when the incident occurred, it could have been even more dangerous if I had been. This is why I stress caution about projecting while in a debilitated state. I will describe the event only to inform you of the possibilities, how to overcome them and, most importantly, how to avoid such an experience.

I awakened briefly in the middle of the night to find my soul guide sitting on my bed. I had known this guide for eleven years and, during that course of time, she had often appeared sitting cross-legged on the side of my bed. So, when this happened, I didn't question it. We spoke briefly about mundane concerns, and then I turned over to go back to sleep. I failed to look her in the eye as I usually did, for looking in the eyes of any spirit is the most sure way of identifying a trickster. There are many spirits who have the hobby of donning familiar forms and faces and who play these roles just for the amusement of trickery. Through the years, I had encountered many of these annoying yet essentially benign entities, but I had learned how to identify the true soul from an impostor by looking at the spirit's eyes. If there was an absence of light energy in the gaze, there was something amiss. A benevolent being always has some amount of beautiful light exuding from the eyes, which truly are mirrors of the soul. However, that night I was half asleep, exhausted, and lazy, so I did not take the time to examine the peepers of this supposedly very familiar face. Just as my soul guide had done countless times when I was ill, the spirit insisted on staying by my side until I went to sleep. Yes, there was a moment or two of an intense gut instinct when I felt uneasy and even questioned why she was being more affectionate than usual. But I was so tired that I shrugged off the intuitive warning.

Just as I fell into light sleep, I felt razor-sharp nails grip my arm with intense force. I woke up panic stricken and could not move my body. In one crushing second I realized that the entity pressed to my back was unlike any I had ever encountered and even doubted the existence of. With indescribable power, it forced its energy into my skin, penetrating me until I felt immobilized and in pain even though this energy invading my body was totally invisible. I struggled with all the strength I had, but to no avail. I tried to pray, but I was so petrified that I couldn't even remember the words. The entity began sucking my energy from my back between the shoulder blades with a loud, unearthly sound while moving against me. The sexual urgency of the frenzied movement seemed to give it additional power, and I actually heard the entity enter my body halfway. It sounded as if an oversized object was being forced into a small suitcase. It was at that moment when rage replaced my fear. How dare this thing use my body! The anger enabled me to begin praying furiously while I imagined my aura burning the entity out of me. After many long moments, which seemed eternal, I finally willed it out. I felt an immediate lightness as it exited with incredible force. It left as quickly as it had seized the opportunity.

Due to the intense prayer and other precautions I took following the attack, the entity never attempted to do it again. But for two months following that night, I often felt its presence. When the attack occurred, I was in the process of relocating, which was fortunate because the move enabled me to break the tie with the environment and the memory of the incident. Though I learned how to protect myself, it was to be a good month before I attempted soul travel again. To this day, I find myself reluctant to fall asleep on my left side or speak to my soul guides at night. The memory and the lingering traces of fear still remain.

True cases of possession are rare, but possession does exist. The very word conjures Hollywood images of demonic seizures and smoldering crucifixes but, beyond the cases of possession that are dramatic enough to be documented and recognized by religious authority, there are possession cases that are unrecorded, more subtle, and that are not validated, even by the victim. These incidents may not seem as frightening or dangerous as a full-blown dramatic possession, but in reality they can be just as harmful.

Just as there are people in the world who strive to do good and those who strive to do the opposite, there are spirits who do the same. Most have once lived on the earth plane, but there are spirits and energies that are created and sustained by the darker forces. Despite many modern schools of metaphysical thought that deny the existence of lower energies and realms, from my own experience, there are forces and realms that are not of the light and are independent from our own inner demons and manifestation of our own fears (Chapter 5 discusses these lower realms). Judging from my negative experiences, there are four types of entities or energies that can cause harm to an individual, especially a soul traveler. Listed below are these four types, followed by techniques to avoid or overcome them.

Tricksters

Tricksters are spirits who do not wish to progress to a higher level of evolvement, yet do not wish to be in a physical body (reincarnate) either. Tricksters are usually bored entities who roam the astral and earth planes looking for a good time, like adolescents on a Saturday night. Their fun is our fear, and their goal is to make humans look like fools so they can get a good laugh. Tricksters are most often harmless, but there are those who break the stereotype. I write this with a light heart, because these cosmic thespians have a biting sense of humor and will do anything to entertain themselves. This includes donning the appearance of our loved ones (living or dead), animals, melodramatic and stereotypical frightening forms such as black-cloaked figures, monsters, et cetera, and especially relish slipping into a costume that resembles our image of a demon. Tricksters have laughed (literally) in my face when I have started to pray in their presence. In fact, only recently have I found the most successful method of getting rid of them. It's very simple and effective most of the time: Laugh at them with all your might. If you're scared, laugh harder. The worst insult to a trickster is not taking them seriously. If you encounter a spirit you believe to be a trickster, laugh, shrug them off, walk away, and forget them. They will persist but, if you stand your ground with a lighthearted approach, they will get bored very quickly and look for entertainment elsewhere. Whether you are in your physical body or your soul body, try this method. On the other hand, if you have a bone-chilling fear, the kind that makes you feel faint, you may be in the presence of an entity that means business. These entities gain more power through our lack of interest in them. If the entity seems more powerful or forcefully enraged by your laughter and dispassion, then chances are you are not dealing with a trickster. If you are not sure, try the laughter method for a serious amount of time. Tricksters usually depart after they see that you are onto them, while other entities tenaciously persist. The only harm a trickster can inflict on you is a wild goose chase and destroying your very important sense of trust. In order to experience beautiful and thrilling journeys out of body, we must keep a sense of trust while leaving room for healthy skepticism. Even if you are mistaken, and the entity is truly your soul guide or a loved one, it is safer to think the worst. If you cause the entity to depart and later learn that the spirit truly was a loved one, he or she will forgive you, so do not be afraid to offend any spirit you feel is not being truthful.

Vicarious Spirits

Vicarious spirits are spirits who have lived on the earth plane but feel that they were not ready for death. They refuse to move on, instead seeking out humans who have similar interests, weaknesses, and experience. In most cases, vicarious spirits are not advocates of either light or dark forces, but are interested in only one thing: fulfillment. Vicarious spirits often experienced unresolved addictions or frustrations while living and seek to live through another person. These spirits will go to any lengths, no matter how long it takes, to influence any living individual. Many clairvoyants can see this type of spirit in bars, sometimes actually hanging on the living while they drink. During my teens a family friend was battling alcoholism and I remember after a few triumphant days of her attempted sobriety, I'd always glimpse a spirit in the house. The spirit was a middle-aged woman, slender and always dressed in clothes of the thirties. Each time I saw her, the smell of sweet wine would fill my nostrils so strongly it was unbearable. And each time I saw her, only hours later, our friend would get exceptionally intoxicated despite her honest effort. I stopped seeing this spirit only after alcoholism ravaged our friend. Some may blame it entirely on the nature of the addiction, but I believe this spirit had much influence on our friend's subconscious mind and was able to discourage the desire for sobriety even more strongly than the disease dictated. I also believe that when the spirit got her fill of vicarious pleasure through this person, she departed, leaving irreconcilable damage.

Eastern teacher Paramahansa Yogananda has explained this very common form of possession as possession of or influence over an individual's subconscious mind. Vicarious spirits are drawn to those of us with similar attractions and fears and, in turn, feed our lower desires and fears so they can find fulfillment through our unconscious submission to their inaudible influence.

Vicarious spirits are perhaps the most dangerous because they are not easily discouraged and are very patient until they see results. Over a period of time, their will is often acted out, and we become less for it. The only way to prevent such a spirit from entering our space is, again, to have a strong and unwavering aura. The best way to get rid of a vicarious spirit is to deal with our own fears and resolve negative temptations. Having excess emotional baggage always attracts these hungry entities; if you should encounter one, either in the physical body or in your soul body, be very willful in thought and action. Let them know that they are not going to get fulfillment through you. Say this aloud with total faith in your sincerity and power. You are the master of your body and mind. No one and no thing can have influence over you unless you believe otherwise. Even if you feel vulnerable to this type of spirit, think strongly and act strongly until you believe you are strong.

If you are unsure you are dealing with such a spirit, consider the following: At unlikely moments, are you tempted to do something that is entirely out of character for you? Do you find yourself drawn to activities, people, and substances that you know are not beneficial to you? Do you go against your better judgment despite all common sense? Do you ever experience overwhelming sexual desire beyond your usual needs that even borders on desperation? If you've answered a definite "yes" to two or more of these questions, you are probably in the presence of a vicarious spirit.

These spirits can have influence over our physical lives and, aside from the dangers of this, they can affect our soul bodies even more profoundly. While out of body we can form many types of relationships with other souls. If you unwittingly form an alliance with a vicarious spirit, they can drain your psychic energy with alarming speed, leaving your physical body open to exhaustion, illness, and depression. The only way to free yourself from this type of spirit is to break all ties with it. Any relationship with a vicarious spirit is intensely emotional or sexual and can make you feel that you cannot live without this other soul. Even living people can act like vicarious spirits and drain our vital energy unintentionally, through stormy emotional ties or sexual experiences. If you experience this type of relationship in your physical body and life, chances are that a vicarious spirit is working through you and the other person.

Incubus and Succubus

The diabolic spirits who raped women, seduced holy men, and sucked the life out of infants in Medieval books gripped the minds of peasants and priests alike and were known as incubi and succubi. Belief in these sexual demons was no laughing matter and reached a feverish peak during the Inquisition. Sexual dreams, nightmares, and the unexplained deaths of babies were all attributed to these creatures of the night.

In our modern age, when science explains all of the above, there are still documented and undocumented cases of spirit molestation. The occult myth of the incubus and succubus (the first being male, the latter female) is not merely the product of the hysterical Medieval mind but a very real astral phenomenon. These spirits gain power and strength through the sexual activity and excesses of the living.

Though these spirits can influence our sexual behavior and feed off of it, there is little danger involving our physical selves—but of course there is the exception. The entity who tried to enter my body was definitely sexually driven. The true danger lies within the astral plane, and the soul body is vulnerable to this type of spirit. Later, I discuss in depth romantic and sexual relationships that are possible through traveling in the spirit body. Due to the possibility of these beautiful partnerships, the soul traveler must always be cautious of the sexually hungry entity who is from the lower realms. The only way to avoid encountering one is proper preparation and wise discrimination. Just because the soul body is free, and there is no need to fear pregnancy, disease, or moral judgment, soul travelers have to make wise decisions just as they would in their physical bodies. This means soul traveling for extraordinary or meaningful love relationships, not for unbridled sexual ecstasy with any willing spirit. Soul traveling merely for sexual quests is dangerous and immediately, without question, attracts lower entities of all kinds. So, to avoid such negative energies, seek higher relationships; you will be surprised to find deep sexual experiences as an added bonus.

Somewhere down the road, if you are out of body and feel an overwhelming sexual attraction to another spirit, act with caution. Blinding sexual desire is usually a danger signal and a warning that the other magnetic soul is aiming to feed off of your energy, for there is no energy quite as powerful as the sexual force. No matter how gripped you are by the attraction, leave the spirit's presence immediately. If you do engage in any sexual activity or melding, you may risk forming a psychic bond or thread with the other spirit, making it possible for the entity to feed from your energy even after you've returned to your physical body and life. This type of attachment can be very draining and dangerous to your emotional, sexual, and spiritual well-being. If you feel that you've made this sort of psychic attachment, I advise you to sever the tie with one of the techniques that will be presented later in this chapter.

Many of these sexually voracious spirits are demonic, very tenacious, and keenly intuitive concerning our sexual desires and repressions. This is why I cannot stress firmly enough the importance of not soul traveling or even attempting to during times of intense sexual needs. If you feel this overwhelming feeling in your physical body prior to projection, resist the temptation of leaving your body because you may already be influenced by such a spirit. This does not mean you are not a spiritual or good person. Anyone from any walk of life can become a target for an incubus or succubus, so the best precaution is to be aware of your own sexuality and to keep it in perspective when considering astral projection and soul travel.

Thought Forms

Every word we think and speak creates an etheric energy form, much the way our breath can be seen on winter days. These thought forms are constantly being created through our words and our ideas. Each thought form carries within it the vibrational energy of the original thought or emotion, so there are positive thought forms as well as negative.

When a clairvoyant sees a thought form or a soul traveler encounters one while out of body, the form appears like a semi-dense mass of smoke. These energies can be of different colors; happy and positive thought forms are usually bright, clear colors such as yellow, blue, rose, or pure crimson while negative energy formed from anger, frustration, and sadness are darkly hued colors such as brown, maroon, muddy yellow-green, and black. Since thought forms are composed of energy and are of astral matter, positive forms are beneficial in that they give back good energy or vibrations. On the other hand, negative thought forms only exude vibrations that are emotionally and physically draining to those in the environment. These negative thought forms can become very thick, build up energy, and eventually take on a life of their own. Independent negative thought energies can become like spirits with individual character, blocking the influx of positive energies into an environment, and thoroughly influencing moods and even behavior of those in their presence. This is why some people find it very difficult being in urban spaces. If all the negative thought forms of any given city could be seen with the naked eye, they would appear as great clouds of black smoke eclipsing most of the positive ones. Poverty, illness, crime, and the frustration of each person's life creates a concentration of mass energy that can weigh down the spirit. This is why it is essential to spend time somewhere in nature as often as possible, where negative thought forms are few and both the person and the environment are cleansed by the pure energy of the elements.

While out of body, you will most probably encounter negative thought forms. Since the soul body is composed of fine etheric matter and thought energies are also of etheric matter, you may experience unpleasant sensations. When I attempted to walk through a negative thought form while in my spirit body, it was like trying to walk through thick layers of a spider's web. The dark energy matter felt sticky, and it reminded me of trying to remove chewing gum from a child's hair. The only way I was able to move through the mass or take it off of my soul body was to think of a very emotionally positive memory. This took time, effort, and proved to be tiring, but once I created a positive thought form that equaled its size and power, the negative energy dissolved.

Thought forms can be harmful to a soul traveler if they cling to the spirit body and are not dissolved before he or she returns to the physical body. When I use the word "harm" I mean that the negativity of the thought energies can build and actually ground the soul body, making subsequent projection difficult if not improbable. So, if you find yourself face to face with a dark energy mass, promptly recall a beautiful memory that makes you feel emotional in a positive way. As you think about the memory, imagine light beaming from your head—light from the pure joy of remembrance. Do this until the thought form dissolves and is replaced by your happy one. If one memory doesn't do the job, think of as many as you wish, but give each one adequate time to produce positive energy.

If you are not sure whether you are in the presence of a negative thought form or a shapeshifting spirit, consider the following: Can you communicate with the energy? Does it send you telepathic messages? If you answered "yes" to these questions, then most likely you are not dealing with a negative thought form, but a genuine spirit. From my own experience, thought forms cannot communicate with us but can be manipulated, empowered, and dictated by us through our own thoughts.

Common Fears

Despite the unpleasant possibilities of traveling in the soul body, with awareness and practice these realities lose their ability to arouse fear. As a soul traveler, my worst obstacle and demon has been my own fear. So remember that one of the most powerful forms of protection is putting fear in its place and knowing that essentially you are the master of your experiences. This means like attracts like, especially within the inner worlds, and having elevated thoughts will catalyze wonderful journeys. However, there are a few concerns many people have regarding astral projection, and I would like to bring these things into clearer focus.

The Silver Cord

There has been much confusion about the existence and function of the silver cord. The silver cord is believed to be an invisible thread that connects the soul to the physical body. Many people who leave the body claim to see this cord, while others declare that they have never seen it. From my own knowledge of this etheric link, the silver cord does exist but it functions differently than expected. We each have a thread of energy that bridges the soul body to the physical body. But instead of functioning as a cord that holds the spirit to the flesh, it acts as a transmitter of cosmic and thought vibration. Through this silver thread we channel energy, knowledge, and guidance from a higher source, though we are unaware of it. Since it does not actually connect the soul to the body, there is no danger of severance—of "losing" the soul while it is away from the physical— nor is death ever a threat. Death cannot result from astral projection or traveling in the soul body. The silver thread of energy known as the silver cord simply dissolves at the time of appointed physical death because it is no longer needed to transfer the above-mentioned information. Finally, it is unnecessary to see the silver cord, so if you cannot "find" yours, it is very normal.

Getting Lost or Stuck

Another area of concern deals with getting lost or stuck in the astral worlds. While out of body, thought is the sole means of transportation. To go anywhere on any plane, the soul traveler simply wills his or her spirit body to the desired destination. Because of this natural ability of the soul, it is impossible to get lost in other worlds. However, if you are out of body and you have a moment of mundane doubt, your thoughts may not be directed properly and immobility may result. The only way a traveler can work free from this situation is to simply remember that thought is the vehicle. Freedom and destination are literally only a thought away. If you find yourself immobile, unable to reach a destination or escape an unpleasant predicament, take a moment to completely relax your mind. Remember the days of your childhood, when pretending was a way of life. Recall your inborn ability to imagine, then direct your thoughts to your desired destination or goal. When all else fails, just think about your physical body and you will automatically return to it.

There were times when I found it difficult to enter my physical body. During those times, I'd slip halfway into my very familiar but dense body and somehow get stuck. When I struggled, I could actually feel physical pain, for half my consciousness was in my soul body while the other half was in the physical. After studying this problem, I realized that I experienced this odd difficulty when my thoughts were not directed and I was thinking in a mundane fashion. For a moment, I forgot I could just walk through solid objects or just drift back into the body's density. As soon as I remembered the realities of the soul's etheric nature, I slipped right into my body like a letter into an envelope. So, if you find yourself in a similar dilemma, remember that even though your soul body feels, looks, thinks, acts, and responds just like your physical self, its true nature enables it to conquer solidity and time.

Frankly, no matter how philosophical you are about death, seeing your physical body on the bed or in the chair with your soul eyes may be unnerving. To this day, sometimes if I touch my physical body while in the projected state, I feel a little spooked. During these times, when the conditioning of society creeps into my solid foundation of spiritual knowledge, I simply remember that I had a soul *before* I had a physical body; that I entered this physical world in spirit form and will leave in spirit form. We are all souls renting the flesh. Everything we taste, touch, smell, see, and hear in this everyday world of earthly experience is leased, including the body. So, when society's uneasiness about death makes me uneasy in the soul body, I remember that all we truly own is the spirit—and owning the spirit is owning all that is infinite.

Lastly, if ever your physical body is in any kind of danger while you are soul traveling, your spirit will instantly return. The soul is at all times intuitively aware of the body's state.

Self-Protection Techniques

Immediately before you attempt astral projection and soul travel, I advise you to use one of the techniques presented here for your self-protection. Even if you are a seasoned traveler, you can never be too protected.

Protection Through Sound

Sound vibration can transform mood, stimulate spiritual and psychic awareness, catalyze healing, and create positive energy that can obstruct negative forces from entering a particular space.

Playing music in the area where you will project is an excellent way to conjure protective and high-vibrational energy. Choose a recording that is uplifting, serene, spiritual, or psychically stimulating, such as Native American drumming or flute music. Avoid rock, jazz, pop, and soul music simply because it tends to ground thoughts as well as the spirit body. Classical is appropriate if it does not provoke sadness or if it is not too modern. Choosing music that makes you feel powerful, spiritual, loving, relaxed, and elevated is important not only because positive energy will spread throughout the area but the aura will respond to the sound vibration. When the aura responds to positive sound, its natural protective abilities are stimulated and increased. When the aura is in the presence of this good energy from sound, it expands, gains power, and grows in brightness and depth of color. When the aura is in this responsive state, no negative energy can trespass its etheric shield of fire.

Creating sound through the direct experience of drumming is perhaps the most powerful way to create protective energies. Choose a drum of any kind, rattles, or even bells or chimes if you prefer those. If you are a musician or singer, you may also play your piano, guitar, cello, flute, et cetera, or sing in the area you plan to project. Positive, beautiful music is very powerful.

Whether you play recorded music or create your own live sound, drench the area with music for twenty minutes or longer prior to projection. Give the sounds time to create positive energy and thought forms. After the music has done its spiritual work, point the index finger of your power hand (the hand you write with) toward the entrance or door of the room you are in. If you are at an outdoor location, point toward the direction of your choice. Imagine that your extended arm and pointed finger are illuminated with white light. Direct all of your thoughts to your arm and finger, feeling powerful. Imagine a beam of white fire leaving the tip of your index finger and reaching the room's entrance or direction you are facing.

31

When you can visualize this light clearly, begin turning clockwise, imagining the projected white light creating a line of psychic fire as you rotate. As you turn, draw a complete circle with this etheric fire in which you will be encased. Know that nothing can violate this barrier you have created. Say aloud in a clear, authoritative voice, "I am protected within this circle. Nothing can harm me, reach me, or influence me. I am a child of the Ultimate Deity and I ask all the spirits of Light to ensure my safety as I embark upon my journey. It is done." When you feel empowered, allow your spoken words to mingle with the sound vibrations created by the music and then proceed with one of the techniques of projection presented in Chapter 4.

Protection Through Angelic Invocation

Angels exist and always will. They are independent from human fads and images and, most of all, they are not owned by any particular religion. Angels are beings of light, composed of the pure essence of the Ultimate Deity. These energies can take many forms on any plane but, as a collective band of helpers, angels govern inspiration, healing, guidance, knowledge and, most of all, protection.

Aside from the many spirit helpers who are assigned to each of us, angel guides are always near. Many times I have seen a bright and shimmering light accompany me on my soul journeys that would vanish when I reached my destination. Protection angels can be consciously invoked before you project, and I personally believe that this technique of self-protection is the most reliable.

Wherever you choose to project, fragrance the area with an appropriate incense. It is widely believed that particular flower essences attract these beautiful beings of protection. Rose, hyacinth, lily of the valley (my own choice), gardenia, and jasmine are only a few you can choose from. Again, be sure your incense is one hundred percent natural for vibrational properties.

As the incense is burning and releasing its delicate perfume, say aloud, "I call on the angelic hierarchy and ask for protection during my journey. Shield me from negative energies and bless me with safety. I call on you, my personal angel guide, to accompany me and be my protector. Thank you, beings of light." After reciting this prayer or something similar of your own choosing, close your eyes and smell the fragrance. Imagine wings of silver light enfolding your body and soul in safety, warmth, and beauty. While you envision this angelic embrace, chant aloud or in your thoughts, "Tahn na zay." This chant was given to me by a soul guide, and it invokes the order of protection angels. Chant these sound-words for five to ten minutes, continuing to feel embraced by beings and wings of light. When you feel ready, proceed with one of the projection techniques presented in Chapter 4.

Protection Through Aura Meditation

This meditation technique can also be used to strengthen the aura on a daily basis, especially during times of depression, fatigue, or illness.

In the area where you plan to project, sit comfortably in a chair or on the floor. Slowly breathe deeply for two minutes or longer, taking full but easy breaths. Allow the flow of air to reach as deeply into the lungs as possible. When you feel that the inhalation of air is deep within your diaphragm, totally relax the chest area and abdomen and hold your breath comfortably for a few long seconds. Gradually exhale the air, remaining as relaxed as possible. When done properly, this type of deep breathing can take you directly into a meditative state that can catalyze out-of-body travel, so after the remainder of this protective meditation you may wish to continue deep breathing and go directly into the "Circular Breathing Projection Technique" discussed in Chapter 4.

After breathing deeply for about two minutes, begin chanting, "Gahn no me try nay." These sound-words stimulate the aura's power of protection and are very effective. Chant for five to ten minutes while imagining rainbow-colored fire surrounding your entire body. Feel the heat generated from your aura's beautiful light; see it expanding with each chant, each breath. Envision your aura projecting outward as far as possible, obstructing all negative energies and keeping your physical and soul body completely safe.

If you chant and visualize for ten minutes or so, you should actually feel a physical sensation of expansion, as if you have wings that are unfurling. This sensation indicates that your aura is indeed in a very vital state and is probably extending much farther than it had been before the meditation. Weak auras can extend only inches from the body, while strong auras can extend outward up to ten feet. The average aura extends six feet away from the body. If done on a daily basis, this meditation can increase your aura's expansion as well as strengthen its protective power to repel unwanted energies and entities.

Once you feel this sensation of expansion after your ten minutes or so of chanting and visualization, proceed with the projection technique of your choice presented in Chapter 4.

Severance

Somewhere down the line, as a soul traveler you may encounter another soul or an entity whom you feel is invading your spiritual space, absorbing your positive energy, or even placing you under psychic attack. If you feel exhausted, drained, depressed, ill, or emotionally tired for no good medical or physical reason, especially after you see a particular spirit, then psychic attack could be the cause. If and when you experience this, you will want to sever the astral tie and break the bond to this spirit. Whether it is the soul of another traveler, a spirit from the inner planes, a lower entity, friend, foe, or lover, the following ceremony of severance is recommended. This technique can be applied even if it is someone in your physical life.

Go somewhere you will not be disturbed, either out of doors or the room in which you practice soul travel. Take along with you an amount of string, twine, or ribbon the length of your arm, a pair of scissors or a knife, and any small physical object that links you to the person or spirit, if any.

Hold an end of the string, twine, or ribbon in each hand as you think intensely of the person or spirit you wish to sever psychic ties with. Remember positive or negative experiences that you've shared with the other. Imagine all that connects you is entering the string and being locked within the fibers. Say aloud, "All that I share with _____ (name of person or spirit, if any) is within this string. All physical, emotional, spiritual, psychic, and sexual (if appropriate) ties no longer connect us, but are in this string." Say this five to ten times with all the willful emotion you can muster. Then take the knife or scissors and say aloud, "With this knife (scissors) I sever all ties with _____ (name of person or spirit, if any). I am protected from, free from, and have no bond with _____ (name) on any plane." Immediately cut the string, twine, or ribbon at the middle point. If you have physical objects made of paper, cut these also into small pieces. If you are outside, bury both pieces of string as well as paper shreds or small objects in soil, leaves, rocks, sand, or stones. If you are indoors, burn the pieces of string as well as any paper shreds in a fireplace or non-flammable container. Whether you are indoors or out, if you have a physical object you cannot cut or burn, promptly throw it in the garbage.

Immediately after the ceremony, take a bath or shower and imagine all traces of the association washing forever down the drain.

If the person is in your physical life, do not see him or her or even talk on the phone. If it is the spirit of another soul traveler, avoid him or her or do not travel for a few days or weeks. If it is an entity, do not travel at all, for any reason, for at least two weeks.

You may have to repeat this severance ceremony several times if the bond is very strong or is re-created, but it will bring results if done with faith and a period of absence on your part is adhered to. Most importantly, know that you are in control and no one and no thing has power or influence over you. Talk to the angels and the Ultimate Deity for guidance.

Chapter Two

Footprints of Light

Traveling with

Soul Guides

*M*y first journey out of the physical body only occurred after I met a soul guide. Though I had grown up in an atmosphere where spirit guides were subjects of casual conversation, the thrill of meeting mine face to face could not have been predicted; nor was it to be predicted how many things I would learn or how my life would change.

*D*estination *does* not measure miles or height;
To soar in the wild embrace of the wind,
The branch of reason, the nest of safety
Must first be betrayed and only then
Will wings know their potential.

Though my psychic ability or second sight came naturally as well as being encouraged and nurtured, I did not fully realize its potential until my teens. I had seen spirits throughout my childhood, knew when I was in someone else's thoughts, and even experienced an extraordinary telepathic relationship with a perceptive English teacher when I was in the sixth grade. But none of these experiences matched contacting my soul guides.

At age fifteen, I asked the Higher Powers to show me who my principal spirit helper was. That same night I dreamed of a spirit woman named Judith. In the dream I saw three photographs of a small, dark-haired woman. When I awakened, I felt I had made a genuine contact of some sort, so I began to speak to this woman, addressing her as Judy. Nightly, before going to sleep, I'd speak to her as if she were listening, and I filled her in on all the melodramatic and catastrophic details of my adolescent life, never listening for an answer. I was content just to have a confidant, invisible or otherwise. Months later, I was boring the poor spirit lady as usual with my nightly outpourings when I suddenly saw a woman sitting cross-legged on the edge of my bed. The lady looked exactly like the Judith in my earlier dream, and I knew by her smiling, beautiful, and patient face that this was Judy. She overlooked my stark surprise and commented on what I had been mentally telling her before her appearance. This conversation lasted for about thirty-five minutes and was to be the beginning of an intense ten-year period of learning and friendship. Through Judy, I learned remote viewing (psychically viewing distant places and people), astral projection, soul travel, and past life self-regression.

The techniques of projection found in this book are based on what I have learned through personal interaction and travel with spirit guides. These guides, in my opinion, can aid a soul traveler immensely by offering protection, being companions during inner world journeys, teaching shamanic skills, and guiding an individual' to realize his or her full spiritual and mystical potential.

Despite the sometimes overused melodrama of "New Age" interests and terms such as spirit guides, such beings exist and are accessible. Within their etheric sphere of existence, these spirits strive to contribute to our human growth and, in turn, grow through catalyzing our emotional and spiritual progress.

Spirit guides or soul guides (as I prefer to call them) can help us travel through the wilderness of spiritual enfoldment and give us support when we travel over the difficult ground of our chosen destinies. They can suggest what areas to travel toward, offer strength in challenging times, and teach us when we are ready. However, soul guides are not givers of reward if we abuse the privilege of interacting with them. Soul guides do not present us with a banquet but rather show us how to plant the seeds, accompany us through the seasons of our labor, and help us gather the harvest by encouraging our inborn qualities of resourcefulness and patience. These helping spirits cannot take us to where we are going in our lives, but they can make the journey less difficult with their wisdom and company.

There are seven types of soul guides who work with each of us through the course of a lifetime. I will describe each and how to consciously make contact with them but, as a rule of thumb, these guides rarely if ever do the following:

- Tell us directly what to do with our lives, give us orders we must follow, or disrespect our free will

- Interfere with our destiny or chosen life lessons; they cannot change what we are meant to experience

- Make lavish promises of power

If ever a spirit does or tries to do any of the above, you are most likely not in contact with a genuine soul guide. When you contact any spirit claiming to be one of your guides, make sure they pass the Genuine Soul Guide Test.

Genuine Soul Guide Test

1. Does he/she/it leave you to your own free will and allow you freedom of choice?

2. Does he/she/it guide, teach, and love you like a model parent would?

3. Does he/she/it strive to make you feel peaceful, spiritually confident, and capable of fulfilling your earthly destiny despite difficulty?

If you answered "yes" to all three, then you are in contact with a true soul guide. If a spirit ever fails the above test, do not pursue contact under any circumstances. Yes, some guides can be very direct with suggestions, have a wise but biting sense of humor, and discipline us as if we were wayward children if need be, but basically their behavior always mirrors the above criteria. No matter how genuine or charming a spirit appears to be, if he/she/it behaves the opposite concerning your well-being, do not pursue the spiritual relationship. If you do make a mistake and the spirit truly is one of your guides, then it will be pleased to see what a wise seeker you are and send another in its stead.

Types of Soul Guides

Each of us has a circle of soul guides who interact with each other, much the same way a group of teachers intermingles to help a student's progress. Some spirits are present during an entire lifetime, while others remain active for shorter periods of time to aid certain situations, relationships, hardships, and the like. Any one of the seven types of soul guides we each have can aid you in soul traveling. These are:

Assigned Guides

Assigned guides are spirits from any plane or planet who are assigned to aid us in particular areas of our lives, from the mundane concerns of everyday living to spiritual progress. Throughout the course of a person's lifetime, an individual may have from two to ten assigned guides. Assigned guides usually have lived an earthly life and, while living, had similar interests, careers, obstacles, and destinies as the person or people they choose to help. These spirits spiritually progress as we progress through their aid, so it is a partnership of learning and growth for both the assigned guide and "student."

Judy was and is one of my principal assigned guides, though others have taken more active roles in recent years. Like Judy, most assigned guides can build very strong and loving bonds with their subjects, therefore a spiritual relationship with such a spirit can be very much like experiencing a deep friendship with a mentor. Due to these ties of kinship, contacting an assigned guide to aid you in astral projection and to accompany you on your journeys can be very rewarding, if not entertaining.

Soul traveling with an assigned guide can give you:

- Mystical knowledge of inner planes

- Companionship

- Introductions to inner plane beings

To contact one of your assigned guides, light a candle before you go to sleep. Say aloud or silently the following prayer: "I ask the Higher Powers of the universe to show me one of my assigned guides in a dream, vision, or a moment of simple knowing. I am ready to meet my teacher and have complete faith. Thank you and thy will be done." Do this nightly until you feel that you've made contact with an assigned guide. Be sure not to overlook contact, for many times the introduction is not dramatic but subtle. If you hear any names pop into your head during any time of the day or night, don't belittle it to your subconscious mind. If you feel a presence, don't be frightened, but talk to it with honesty. Above all, however your guide contacts you, trust your psychic impressions and believe in your inborn mediumistic abilities. Remember that the truest and most profound of mediums do not channel by letting a spirit into their physical body while the entity speaks through their vocal cords, but rather by simply listening to the inner voice. Yes, many mediums truly channel by divine possession, but this psychic gift is not better, truer, or more reliable than other mediumistic gifts. Strive to find your own unique and profound way of communicating with the unseen by having faith and patience. It will happen.

Ancestor Guides

Ancestor guides are highly revered in shamanic cultures and are an important element in the magical religions of Africa and their offshoots. This type of soul guide can be very powerful in their assistance if the ancestor spirit has reached a certain level of evolvement beyond the threshold of death.

When a family member passes into the next world, he or she begins a cycle of spiritual progress until the soul essence becomes purified through evolvement. This may happen when the last incarnation on earth is completed or between incarnations. When this happens, a familial spirit may choose to solely focus on a family member to help him or her reach their spiritual potential. Many people automatically assume that deceased loved ones can predict our futures, intervene in our daily lives, or possess supernatural powers, but simply leaving the earth through death does not give a spirit these powers unless they are learned, cultivated, or earned within the inner worlds. But within each family, evolved familial spirits do work and strive to aid their kin, especially if the spirit was spiritual, religious, or a practicing magician while living.

Working and traveling with an ancestor guide can be very rewarding, for sharing the same blood or emotional energy makes the bond between guide and subject profound. Contacting an ancestor guide can give you:

- Strength, empowerment, and shamanic abilities in the physical world as well as the inner planes

- Deeper understanding of your inner divine self through spiritual intimacy with a guide from your own bloodline

- Team results from guide–subject spiritual efforts when living family members need healing, guidance, et cetera

To contact an ancestor guide, you may wish to focus on a deceased family member of your choice to whom you feel a special connection or simply leave it to the Higher Powers to make the choice for you. If you do not know your true biological roots, your request will still be heard and granted. If you are adopted, you may make contact with an ancestor from either your biological or foster family's bloodline. The emotional bloodline of unrelated family members is often stronger than those genetically bonded, so do not worry if your family history is different.

If you have an ancestor in mind, place any photographs or personal articles of the family member in the immediate area where you will send out your request. You may wish to hold one of the articles or simply write down the ancestor's name on a piece of paper and hold that. If you do not know who you are contacting, simply concentrate on your image of an ancestor guide, whatever it may be (for example, you may wish to envision him or her in period clothing). Either way, light a candle and say the following prayer: "I ask the Higher Powers of the universe to help me make contact with an ancestor guide, (insert the name of a family member if it is known), to accompany me on my inner world journeys. Please show me in a dream, vision, or moment of knowing which familial spirit is guiding me at this time. I ask this in the name of the Ultimate Deity and the power of my bloodline. Thy will be done."

When this prayer request is done daily, you will notice some sort of contact transpiring most likely in the dream state. Again, take all "random" thoughts, images, voices, and dreams seriously. Look for subtle, rather than dramatic, communication between the worlds. Trust your inner divine self to show you the way.

Angelic Guides

Each of us, over the course of a lifetime, has approximately three angelic guides working behind the scenes for our well-being. These divine intelligences are the purest of soul guides.

Contact with an angelic guide is usually dramatic in the early stages and then can become as subtle as a whisper. My first contact with a guiding angel occurred in the dream state when I was lucid dreaming (being consciously aware during dreaming). This initial introduction was the beginning of a series of intense dreams and visions that ushered me into the supernatural realm of spirituality. I have heard the thundering voice of my guiding angel and received his vivid images telepathically, but I have never come face to face with him in the way other soul guides have come to me. Yes, angelic guides occasionally don physical forms and images to communicate with us, but most often they are very elusive in appearance and prefer to manifest through vibrant color and sound energy. While out of body, I have seen my angelic guide as a beautiful silver-white light energy that looks like a sphere of pristine fire burning near my shoulder as I travel. Doing his protective duty, he disappears as soon as I reach my destination. I do not always see this angelic light accompany me but, when I need additional protection, it always appears without my asking.

Angelic guides are closest to us. When our other soul guides have business to attend to within the inner worlds, they temporarily leave us, but our angelic guides are always near. Due to this loyalty, traveling with angels assures the utmost safety of the soul traveler. Since at least one out of the three always-present angelic guides has been with an individual for over a period of lifetimes and has seen the individual soul through the reincarnation process, making contact with one is easy because the bond has already been established on a higher level.

Contacting and traveling with your angelic guides can give you:

- Guaranteed protection during journeys

- Supernatural experiences beyond the physical senses

- Clearer understanding of your purpose in this lifetime

To contact your angelic guides, before sleep and on rising, light a candle and say the following prayer: "In the name of Archangel Michael, I ask the Higher Powers of the universe to bring me into contact with my angelic guides. I ask the angels to accompany me on my inner world journeys to protect me and show me the wonders of creation. I thank you, angelic guides, for your constant presence. Thy will be done."

As stated before, angels communicate and manifest most often through color and sound, so if you are drifting into sleep one night and you see an array of vibrant colors in your mind's eye, know that you are making angelic contact. If you hear extraordinarily beautiful music coming from an unknown source, your angelic guides are inviting you into their sphere of energy, or you may be one of the chosen few who will see their angelic guides manifest in their most dramatic celestial costume, with upsweeping streams of light energy that resemble bird's wings. Have faith and you will enjoy angelic experiences you will never forget, however dramatic, however subtle.

Animal Power Guides

Each person is spiritually linked to certain members of the animal kingdom. Each animal has vibrational power that can aid us in healing, spirit journeys, and self-knowledge. Shamanic cultures have always recognized animal powers; shamans embark upon the vision quest and spirit journey with the aid of these guiding spirits. The average, modern-day individual is no exception.

Each individual has one to four animal power guides. These guides become most active when we are in need of stability or grounding, physical energy, or psychic strength. Calling on these animal intelligences to aid you in astral projection and protection can be very rewarding in a short amount of time. During a time of illness, I called on the cheetah, one of my principal animal power guides. After five minutes or so of mentally repeating the word "cheetah," the haunting face of this great cat appeared in my mind's eye. It stared at me with great intensity until I felt a flow of energy connecting the two of us in mystical kinship. I continued to recite "cheetah" until a wave of psychic strength began to transform the physical sickness I was experiencing. When this psychic energy wave crested, I projected my consciousness into the moving body of the cheetah. This was no ordinary visualization. I *was* the cheetah. I forgot what it was like to have a human body as my consciousness slipped into the cat's. Suddenly, I had four legs, a tail, and was running at rapid speed through a sea of tall grasses. I raced with the wind, exuberant, ecstatic, one with the earth and completely ignorant of the concept of time. Just as I really began to enjoy this new state of being, I was back in my familiar two-legged body and thoroughly healed of my ailment.

Working with an animal power guide can make projection easier for many people (this technique will be discussed in Chapter 4). To contact your principal animal power guide for any purpose, especially as a preparation for projection, think of the animals you are particularly drawn to. Which animal gives you a burst of joy when you see it? Which animal often appears in your dreams? Which animal do you identify with? Which animal are you terrified of? Yes, that last question could be very significant. Snakes have been my greatest personal fear since my earliest memory, and I have been haunted by them periodically in my dreams. So I was very surprised to find that the water snake is one of my animal power guides.

When we have an animal power that frightens us this way, the intelligence can either represent qualities within us that must be cultivated or darker aspects of ourselves that must be examined and finally conquered. Most intimidating animal powers teach lessons of self-protection, defense when needed, and discipline. If such a power comes to you, take things in stride and work with it. You could learn your greatest lessons there.

Once you have a few animals in mind that attract you, choose to focus on the one you prefer more than the others. Even if you have a fascination with spiders, lizards, or scorpions, follow your affection. All creatures hold different types of power and are all equal in importance, validation, and spiritual significance.

To focus on an animal power, you may find magazine clippings, photographs, or paintings of the animal, or watch nature documentaries. Once you feel familiar with a particular power, find a quiet spot, outdoors if possible. Recite the name of the animal aloud or silently until you see pictures in your mind's eye or even sense an invisible presence beside you. If another animal comes into focus other than the one you are trying to contact, pursue that one. Make time as often as possible to sit with your animal power. Tell it your physical or psychic needs. Watch for dreams, mental pictures, random ideas or visions, voices, or "coincidences." Contact will probably be established quicker than with other soul guides because we share the same planet with animal powers and we depend on one another for survival and well-being. We have a group learning experience with all creatures who share the earth with us.

Elemental Guides

Just as there are creatures of the earth, air, water, and fire, there are invisible energies of these elements that live within them and are etherically composed of the elements themselves. Because we could not live without earth, air, water, and fire, we are equally linked to the elements and the beings within them.

Each individual is spiritually linked to these elements and has one to three elemental guides as well. Elemental guides are the most elusive of the soul guides, but this does not mean that they are less active than the others. These guides primarily work with our emotional and mental natures and are so close to our individual experience that they literally share our consciousness.

Working with an elemental guide can help us stabilize emotion and guide us on fantastic journeys through the etheric kingdoms of nature while out of body. An elemental guide can part the veil between the physical, pragmatic worlds and the inner realms shimmering with nature spirits, fire beings, water nymphs, and strange life forms resembling semi-divine creatures of Greek mythology. With such a guide, you can travel within these realms with total protection and learn how to interact with these astral species as if you are one of them.

To contact an elemental guide, think of the element you feel most akin to. Use your interests as a compass. Do you still have a childish passion for mermaids or fairies? If you feel drawn to fire, sit by the hearth or a candle and talk to the beings within the flames. Invite your elemental guide into your waking consciousness, asking it to escort you through the invisible realms of the natural world when you are out of body. The same for water. When you are by the sea or even taking a shower, talk to the beautiful beings of the waters. When you are in a garden or in a forest, talk to the earth spirits. When you are on a mountain summit or in the path of the winds before a storm, speak to the inhabitants of the air. Elemental guides will always listen to someone who befriends them with respect, and they will always offer their knowledge when pursued with gentleness, humility, and faith.

Deities

The Ultimate Deity or God force, the Higher Power responsible for the creation of all the worlds unknown and known, manifests in infinite possibilities. Deities, gods, and goddesses are the many faces of the One. These deities have many facets of being that may be contacted by the soul traveler whose wings are rooted in faith. As a traveler between worlds, the following deities may be of importance to you:

- Agasgaminam (Jain, Lord of Astral Travelers)
- Isis (Egyptian Goddess and Lady of Magical Arts)
- Artemis (Greek Goddess of Women, Protection, and Elemental Kingdoms)
- Hermes (Greek God of Travelers and Communication Between Worlds)
- Dionysus (Greek God of Ecstasy)
- Genesha (Hindu God of Wisdom and Remover of Obstacles)

There are countless facets of the Divine that may be called upon. The list above are energies that have helped me as a soul traveler.

Can a deity really manifest and guide you? Yes, if your intention is pure and your faith is unwavering. Be sure to take time to pray or speak with your chosen deity as often as possible. Ask for guidance and contact. When you are ready, it will happen. Whether you actually see or hear the deity doesn't matter. When called on, the Divine Energy is always present.

Helpers

Helpers are spirits who assist any of the soul guides in service, contact, et cetera. Helpers are only present for as long as they are needed, then they move on. They can temporarily serve as guides if the need arises. When you contact any soul guide, you automatically contact helpers also. These gracious spirits often help out with our earthly desires and wishes. If you have a wish or a small dream that you believe is too trivial for your soul guides, ask your helpers. They have the joy of children and instinctively know our heart's desires and try to fulfill them if we don't get too greedy and abuse the privilege. In the future, if you are out of body and have such a wish that can be fulfilled while in the projected state, call on a helper. If you are in your physical body and need help in locating an object, book, person, et cetera, ask a helper. They don't like fluffy, indirect requests, so be sure to come out and say what you want. Talk to them as if you were talking to a friend who can help.

Soul guides may be contacted before projection or while you are in the projected state. You may not meet your guides until you are out of body, so if you don't make profound contact until you are out of the physical body, don't get discouraged and think that no one is out there.

Whenever you are in need, out of body or otherwise, your soul guides will be present. All you have to do is acknowledge them. This bond is unconditional.

All soul guides work with the eternal part of our soul essence, called the higher self. This self is the intelligence of our divine self, the part of ourselves who chose the life we are now experiencing. So do not worry if your conscious self interacts with your soul guides directly, for your higher self is in constant contact with them. Your higher self, therefore, is the ultimate guide and knows the needs and desires of your soul now clothed in your physical body. This self is the spark of the Ultimate Deity, so, if you wish, you may simply call on the all-knowing and all-seeing part of you as well as your soul guides. Contacting your higher self can increase the clarity of your psychic awareness as well as stimulate your inborn spiritual ability to experience cosmic consciousness or complete oneness with all things, all worlds, all energies.

When you enter the world of soul guides, you will realize, like never before, that we are never alone. At our darkest hour or most brilliant moment of triumph, we are lovingly cradled by the Invisibles.

Chapter Three

The Lives of a Soul

The Nature and Abilities

of the Spirit Body

During a particular astral projection workshop, I led a small group through a preliminary meditation. Everyone chose an area on the floor and attempted to leave their physical bodies. After the exercise, each person described their experience, whether they were successful or not. One woman calmly described how she had spent the twenty-minute period floating through the stars. According to her, she had never consciously left her body until that night, yet her description was very vague and her overall experience sounded like a pleasant but insignificant daydream. Yes, I believe a part of

It is then

The Soul will hear the litany of the winds

And will look above its own greatness

To the stars

And know which ones are the lanterns

Of the Gods.

her consciousness had entered another level of experience, perhaps within her own psyche, but judging from my own experience and the experience of others, a true out-of-body journey is dramatically different from the meditative state that this woman described.

When the soul or consciousness leaves the physical body successfully, it is a vivid, crystalline experience. Aside from the lightness of being that is experienced, there is little if any difference between being conscious in the physical body and being conscious in the spirit body. For example, one morning when my mother awakened, got up, and proceeded to get dressed for work, she casually glanced toward the bed and saw her physical body still resting. She had been out of body, yet the sensation and act of beginning the day had been identical as the actual physical routine! So you see, "floating through the stars" during a true soul journey would be like traveling through space in the physical body minus the limitations and space training, which would leave an indelible and ecstatic sense of reality on the traveler.

Many people ask, "But how will I know if I'm successful? What does it really feel like? What can I do? Can I eat, make love, run? Will I be just a floating haze? What will I look like?" Hopefully, this chapter will give you a dynamic portrait of what a soul traveler can do.

Sensation

Every bone, muscle, organ, nerve, mole, scar, and characteristic of your physical self is imprinted on your soul body. This means that the spirit is an identical copy of your flesh. The spirit self has all of the physical five senses we use every day, even if one particular sense is impaired in your physical life. For example, if you have loss of sight, hearing, or the use of a limb in your physical body, your spirit will not retain this limitation. While out of body, the blind can see, the deaf can hear, and those who are wheelchair-bound can run through fields. The challenges we face in physical living have no influence over the spirit's timeless and complete form.

Not only are the five daily senses retained, but they are often heightened. Due to physical, mental, and emotional complications of our everyday, stressful lives, our senses are not always keenly responsive unless we find a few moments of clarity and peace during spiritual contemplation, lovemaking, or creative work. However, in the spirit body, we are less bound by all of the factors that can contribute to these physical periods of numbness. Out of the body's cocoon, we can fully realize the potential of feeling. How an athlete feels during a runner's high or an artist feels at the zenith of creative inspiration can most accurately describe the senses of the spirit in the projected state. Everything is extraordinarily and ecstatically real, the way life appeared to us in early childhood before daily demands numbed our sensitivity with a protective callus.

The spirit body feels heat and cold, but is able to adapt to temperature by will. If you project to a snowy forest in the middle of a blizzard, you have the choice of experiencing the cold with discomfort but no harm to your "body," or simply willing yourself into a state of perfect adaptation. All you need to do is think of the desired state of comfort. Once you do this very simple act of thought, you can walk barefoot through snowdrifts without being subject to freezing temperatures. Adapting to the environment in this way will not alter the experience of walking through a winter wilderness; it will only give you another level of experience.

Astral sight (the sense of sight while in the spirit body) has another dimension of ability. Not only can you see with perfect vision, but you will have the ability to "see" behind you. This is not as obvious or confusing as it sounds, but rather is a very natural sensation of knowing at all times what is around and behind you, a sense of visual knowing. Like adapting yourself to temperature by thought or will, you can also choose to see the etheric life forms and energies within nature that would ordinarily be invisible to the physical, naked eye. Spirits of the trees, flowers, mountains, heavens, and waters can be observed with astral sight.

While out of body, you have the ability to walk, run, swim, skip, jump, and dance. Any movement the physical body can do, so can the spirit body. The most exciting thing you can do in spirit form that you cannot do physically is soar. Just by will, you have the option to fly, drift, hover, spin, walk on water, tiptoe on the leaves of a towering tree, breathe under the waves as you swim, and any impossible activity you once dreamed of doing as a child.

Yes, you do bring all of your fears with you into the spirit world, so if you have a phobia concerning water or heights, you may have trouble succeeding with the above until you learn how to discard the fear. Having had a serious fear of water all of my life, it took me awhile to learn the ways of the soul body in this area. I would dive into shimmering pools of sunlit water, sure that I had conquered the fear, but as soon as I remembered the phobia I would begin to experience a choking sensation that would have me rise desperately to the surface to breathe. As long as I remember the nature of the soul and not to think in physical terms, I am able to enjoy journeying through water. So, if you find yourself soaring through blue skies and suddenly experience fear and a sense of limitation, immediately remember that your physical body and mind have no hold over your spirit. Your thoughts guide your soul body. Think that you have no fear. Think that you can fly and you will! It is more than possible to face your fears in the soul body and eventually overcome them in your physical life as well. Working with such phobias while out of body can be inexpensive and positive therapy that, with time, will bring you onto the same level with your fears and free you from their grip.

During the first few times of conscious projection, mental limitation may be a problem. For example, you may try to walk through a wall and get "stuck." (Don't laugh, it does happen!) I remember one time I tried to pass through such a wall when I suddenly thought, *I can't do it!*—and I literally got lodged within the fibers of the wood. I struggled. I wrestled. I panicked. I couldn't breathe . . . then I said to myself, "Hey, stupid, you are not physically in the wall—walk through it!" So, with this simple but difficult realization, I passed through the wall . . . and did it four more times because it was such fun.

Another area of difficulty may be in remaining grounded. Sometimes you might feel like a balloon, unable to stay stationary for a length of time. If you experience this sometimes annoying bopping sensation, imagine there are weights in each of your feet. Feel and think that you are anchored, and you will be.

But you are probably asking, "How will I know if I'm successful and not just having a vivid dream or imaginary trip?" As soon as you leave the physical body, you will immediately, without question, feel light, airy, weightless. This euphoric sensation of having "no bones" will amaze you every time you are successful and completely projected. This experience and state of freedom is the primary indicator that you are truly in your spirit body. In case you are still a skeptic, look for your physical self, the envelope you slipped out of. If you have projected to another room or location entirely, then enjoy your trip. In this case, you will see your physical self when you return to it. Otherwise, if you go looking for the physical body, you may automatically be drawn back into it before you've had a chance to explore. In essence, when you are free from the physical body and conscious in your spirit form, there will be no question whether you have been successful. If doubt arises, then most likely you did not experience a true projection.

$\mathcal{A}ppearance$

As explained earlier, the soul body is a direct copy of your physical self. When you initially leave the physical body, you will have every characteristic of your everyday self—freckles, dimples and all. When you meet someone else who is also out of body or any other spirit, you will appear as such unless you choose to change your form.

Since the direction of thought begets adaptation and transportation of the soul body, it also can transform your appearance. For example, if you wish to completely experience being in the weightless state, you may imagine that you are simply spiritual matter. When you think yourself into this state of being, you will be formless. When you choose to travel in this way, you will most likely appear semi-transparent: softly hued gossamer that barely glimmers with the slightest silver. Changing back into your physical appearance is as easy as willing it. Think of it as mentally changing clothes. If you must, you can also lose some unwanted pounds, change your hairstyle, et cetera. But bear in mind that the inner worlds can be misleading. If and when you meet a friend or partner in these realms, you will want to be as honest as you would want him or her to be. So, my advice is to change your daily image within reason and not think that being out of body can be free cosmetic surgery, so to speak. Once this gets out of control, the true essence of spirit travel can become lost and be no different than physical life with its petty vanities.

This doesn't mean you cannot experiment or shed some physical characteristic that you wish to be free of temporarily. During my early twenties, I was going through the ordeal of orthodontics and experienced pain on a daily basis. Each time I projected over the three and a half years of tooth straightening, I automatically removed the braces in my soul body. Needless to say, this relief saw me through the difficult times. The same approach can apply to minor illness. If you have a cold, for example, you can immediately eliminate it astrally. If you are chronically ill, please take precaution. As I said earlier, illness can weaken the aura's defense, inviting unpleasant energies. However, if you use the suggested aura-protection techniques, soul travel can give you time to feel healthy and even catalyze major physical healing. Spiritual healings can occur, but they are not obedient to thought or will alone. A Higher Power can create a dramatic healing, but it is most often a gift.

Sometimes, due to injury, deformity, or illness, thought forms can collect within the soul body. A person who has chronic pain or who is unable to walk, for instance, may carry the physical ailment with them into the inner worlds. It may be difficult to will the illness or limitation away, and it may take time to dissolve the thought energies that have built up. If you should experience this, keep trying. Imagine, visualize, and direct your thoughts to wholeness.

I have seen this process unfold by observing those who have passed on. I remember one particular man who had spent his entire life in a mental institution. Even though he was in the beautiful afterlife in his spirit form, he could not let go of the mental agonies he experienced while living. The same situation applied to an elderly woman who could not "walk" because thought forms had collected to such etheric density due to leg problems while she was living. With my soul guides, I learned how to work with these spirits and show them how to clear their own obstacles so they could move on. When thought forms distort the soul body in this way, a spirit has trouble contacting their soul guides or even finding the inner worlds. These spirits usually become accustomed to drifting about the earth plane, hence the numerous reported hauntings by ghosts such as "One-eyed Jack" or "Limping Charlie." This sounds humorous, but the spirit trapped within its own web-like thought forms spun by fear, pain, or trauma is very unhappy and lost. So, the bottom line is this: The more difficulty you have willing your own appearance or well-being, the more thought forms you have to dissolve. Over time, with patience and true positive thought direction, you can surmount even the most stubborn obstacles associated with the self.

Lastly, but most importantly, the ability to change into any desired form should not be used to terrorize, mislead, or trick any other spirit. Have fun, but never forget the Golden Rule. On the other side of the coin, be cautious yourself of such dramatics. Remember to look into the eyes of any spirit in question. Your "gut" will tell you if he/she/it is on the level or not. If you have any doubts, move on. Game playing can get very unpleasant in the inner worlds, so it is best to avoid these situations no matter how tempting it may be to participate. If you need to change form and image for self-protection (to confuse or throw off a mischievous energy), then don't hesitate. It's like carrying mace. You have the option if you need it.

Vibrational Interaction

"So if your mother was in her soul body, how did she get dressed?" you may be asking. It's a simple answer. Each physical object—including furniture, appliances, food, books, and any other thing you can think of that does not have a "living" soul—has an etheric counterpart. This etheric counterpart has an astral self, a vibration that can intermingle with your spirit body. For instance, if you find your soul body in Paris and you want to sample that wonderful croissant on the bakery shelf, you simply pick up the croissant as if you were there physically. Of course, the physical croissant will not be moved, but its vibrational essence will be. Use the same technique if you want to eat the croissant at one of the little tables outside. You simply would move the chair to sit down as if you were there physically. Again, the actual chair would remain in its physical, stationary position, but its vibration would be moved at your command.

This ability to relate to the vibrational form of physical objects gives the soul traveler an infinite number of experiences to sample. Someone once asked me if it was possible to eat in the projected state. When I explained to him that even eating is possible, he automatically assumed that the entire experience would be vague and barely remembered, if at all savored. Contrary to his assumption, eating, like any other activity experienced out of body, is enjoyable and vivid. It is only a matter of interacting with the essence of physical food.

For a time, I found it thrilling to journey to the Bahamas and often walked through the colorful markets. A friend in my physical life had taken an extensive trip to the same areas where I explored astrally. Of course, he had no idea of my double life, but as we discussed the Caribbean, he took it for granted I had also taken a (physical) journey. He was very surprised to find that I had never gone to the Bahamas and asked me how I knew so much about the place. I told him I read travel guides for mental vacations! So you see, going to the straw markets and trying on hats for the heck of it in my soul body proved to be probably more enjoyable than my friend's physical trip involving expenses, transportation, and hassles. Working with astral vibrations can give you a wonderful taste of distant cultures without the risk of spending a fortune, getting food poisoning, and losing your luggage. Soul traveling could put the travel industry out of business because of its simplicity (but we'll keep this a secret).

Astral activity is not limited to the earth plane. The most ecstatic journeys are the ones taken within the inner worlds above the earth plane (these many planes of existences of heart-stopping beauty and how to travel there will be discussed in depth in Chapter 5).

As a final rule of thumb concerning vibrational interaction, remember that nearly anything you can do physically, you can do astrally. Feel as if you are doing it physically, and the process of working with vibrational forms will be automatic.

Time

While you are traveling within the earth plane (our physical planet and universe), you will be aware of light, dark, and the cycles of the day. This makes it possible to watch the sun rise over the Ganges in India or witness meteor showers over the desert in the southwestern United States. If I have a certain activity in mind involving certain times of the day, I check time zones throughout the world. This makes it possible to plan projection to catch a performance of the kabuki theater in Japan or a fireworks display in New York City. However, the importance of time loses its power once we are out of body. A few hours in the projected state can feel like a few moments, a half hour at the most. However, upon returning, you may feel as if you've been gone for a long period of time.

When traveling within the inner worlds beyond the earth plane, time does not exist. Perhaps this is the most profound realization that soul travelers experience while exploring these hidden planes of finer existence. Time is a human concept and is totally meaningless once you travel beyond the physical plane. The freedom of this simple but shattering knowledge is joyous, and its remembrance can be carried back into daily living when the mundane bridle of routine circles us around the clock. Suddenly, we allow ourselves to slow down, at least inside of our own minds. Observing time out of body brings it all into perspective.

This subject brings us to the next question: "How long can you remain out of body?" There is no set rule on the time period of projection. Personally, I have never consciously traveled in my soul body for a period longer than two and half hours. However, I have traveled in my soul body in the dream state (during sleep) for almost four hours. Each individual is different but, when projection is accomplished while you are awake, the time period of travel is shorter than nocturnal dream state journeys due to the schedule and distraction of daily living. Interrupted concentration, a neighbor's dog barking, a passing car, or fatigue can shorten or conclude the projection.

Lastly, it is possible to travel back into time, but it may take practice. You can travel back into your former lives or historical events, but you will not be able to interact with any individuals or change any event that has transpired. When you travel back into time, you are going within the thought forms and memories of events that are imprinted upon the collective mind or consciousness of the earth. Past events have etheric selves, existing memory forms that can be relived.

Emotions

When out of body, many soul travelers claim to feel emotion more deeply than they do in their physical lives. This is because the astral world is the realm of emotion. All of humanity's negative and positive feelings are collected within the astral plane as thought forms. This intensity of emotion can be misleading and even spiritually dangerous, especially when you form astral partnerships while out of body. The finer inner worlds are beyond this astral storage house of feelings, so it is important to strive to project to these higher realms when journeying within the inner worlds.

When you travel within the earth plane, you can meet others who are out of body and also living like yourself. These travelers may be aware or unaware of their journeys. Due to the freedom that is experienced in the soul body, as well as the anonymity, tapping into our often-buried emotional intensity is easy and non-threatening. It is very easy to form attachments (sometimes not beneficial), throw caution to the winds romantically or sexually, and to skip all of the common preliminaries of getting to know another person. When this happens to you as a soul traveler, you can get into deeper waters than expected. "It's not like I have to live with the person or even see him/her again if I don't feel like it," you may say to yourself, but a few weeks, months, or even years down the road, you find yourself still involved or hassled by a clinging partner or friend. No, you don't have to live with this person, nor are you obligated to sustain a relationship of any nature, but you have one thing you probably did not consider: astral or psychic bonding. Unfortunately, you cannot write a "Dear John or Jane" letter, drop off the key, and get on with your life, as you would in a physical relationship. Be cautious in forming relationships on impulse, including sexual encounters. If you find yourself in one of these situations, I advise you to use the severance technique in Chapter 1.

Despite the freedom of feeling in the soul body, many of us still carry emotional baggage with us even into the projected state. Because of this, emotional ties can be very much like physical life. From my own experience, I suggest that you test the waters before diving into any relationship, even non-sexual. Meeting someone astrally is like having a buzz from a wonderful wine on a summer night: everything is beautiful. But when the buzz wears off, you remember the mosquitoes. If you feel very emotional toward someone on meeting them, take time to find out why before you hand over your heart. It is no different than what we should do in our daily lives. Your soul mate or soul brother/sister is out there somewhere, but don't assume that each person you feel an instant emotional attachment to is that person. Many times when we feel sudden emotion or sexual energy, we are absorbing the other person's reaction to us. This visceral osmosis can be rapid in the soul body and the astral world with which the earth plane is interlocked. With experience, you will be able to distinguish between true soulful attraction and the whimsical flurry of the moment.

Relationships, the inner worlds, and the sacred sexuality of the physical and spirit bodies will all be thoroughly explored later in this book. For now, let's get to the root of the matter: techniques of projection!

Chapter Four

Breaking the Bonds of Flesh

Techniques of

Conscious Projection

*O*nce you learn how to consciously leave the physical body, generally the ability must be nurtured and maintained. The gift of astral projection can never be lost, but it must be practiced in order for an individual to reach his or her potential as a soul traveler.

Straight and unfailing as an arrow,
I leave the impoverished safety of the bow;
Unconquered, in triumph's ascent
I soar into the eagle's ecstasy.

From my own experience, it is like driving a car. Once you learn to drive well, you never forget; however, weather, state of mind, time of day, outside circumstances, and environment all affect your driving. These same factors play

Most Common Cultural Methods of Astral and Conscious Projection

Culture	Method
Tribal Nations	Hallucinogens
	Trance-dance
	Drumming
	Chanting
Eastern Ascetics	Deep meditation
	Yoga
	Hunger, thirst
	Sleep deprivation
	Pain infliction
Islamic Sufis	Trance-dance
	Spinning
Greek Initiates	Training in the Eleusinian Rites
European Wiccans	Flying ointments
	Mystical herbs

an important role in cultivating a rich soul traveler's lifestyle, and are often the reason why many people fail to progress after the initial projection. It is common for an individual to have one or two successful out-of-body journeys and then few if any sojourns thereafter. The only way to avoid this frustration is to experiment with more than one projection technique. One or two techniques will most probably net you good results, while one or more may not work for you at all. Often, due to factors comparable to driving, your tried and true technique may fail one day, while another that has never been useful will bring you success.

Before trying any of the techniques in this book, I suggest you read through each one presented. Don't get discouraged if you fail the first time or even the twentieth time. Leaving the body is a process of discovery, even if you have the inborn gift of astral projection. No matter how easy or difficult this spiritual art is for you, give yourself time to fully realize your potential.

As you embark on your quest, here are some reminders:

- Attempt projection only between meals,
  when you are not hungry or too full

- Choose a time to project when you will not be disturbed
  by people, phones, barking dogs, et cetera

- Always meditate, engage in positive ritual, or pray
  before attempting to project (see Chapter 1)

- Never attempt projection during times of intense
  emotional upset, illness, or sexual frustration

Coming out of the projection mode of consciousness and returning to the physical body is as important as entering the state and leaving the body. Here are three tips for a comfortable return and adjustment to physical surroundings:

1. At the end of your journey, you will automatically return to your physical body and enter with ease; sometimes you may have trouble entering. If this should happen, simply remember your spirit's triumph over physical density. You can never be "stuck."

2. Always remain in the reclining or seated position you have chosen for projection for at least ten minutes after you return or come out of the trance state.

3. Do not attempt to do hard physical work or play for at least thirty to forty minutes after a successful projection; re-adjusting too quickly to physical surroundings can give you a headache, nausea, nervousness, or mood swings.

During the course of your experience, you may wish to keep a journal to record all of your attempts, techniques, results, journeys, et cetera. If you don't have the time or the inclination to write it by hand, don't forget that you can use a typewriter or computer. Or, perhaps, you may wish to record your experiences on cassette.

As a final note, remember that your experience of projection may not be identical to mine. Each soul is unique, so you may even wish to add elements to your chosen technique. Feel free to experiment and be creative.

Techniques of Projection

The Solar Plexus Technique

The solar plexus technique is a commonly experienced and instructed way of astral projection. Many people find this technique to be reliable, while others find it unsatisfactory or even unpleasant.

If you have a sensitive nervous system, you may find this way of projection unsettling. You may experience a headache, rapid heartbeat, and upset stomach, but don't rule it out if you haven't tried it. It is good to try all of the techniques here to find which is best suited for you.

Intense emotion can surface while using the solar plexus gateway due to the fact that the solar plexus center is an etheric storagehouse of all positive and negative memories of an individual. All feelings, fears, and desires are collected in this area.

Anyone using this technique with intense emotion, especially negative, may find that his or her journey is limited to the lower astral plane. The lower astral is the plane of illusion and shapeshifting entities and energies. Often when you travel to this plane, which is very close to the physical plane, you may find that your soul body is unable to travel beyond this lower astral and into the finer spiritual realms. However, if you have no significant emotional baggage, depression, anger, physical or mental fatigue, or unresolved sexual issues, you will have positive experiences using the solar plexus technique.

To begin, deep breathe for a few long moments. Once you can deep breathe without mental or physical effort and your breathing falls into a languid, unbroken pattern, take considerable time to experience the intake of air traveling all the way down to your diaphragm. Continue to breathe, being aware only of the air flowing into your solar plexus region. If other thoughts pop into your head, allow them to enter your consciousness and then pass through. Don't hold onto any thought, including thoughts about the anticipated projection. If you constantly remain aware of leaving the body, you will net no results. The breathing process must be allowed to take you into a meditative state where you will be oblivious to the past and future and only be cognizant of the moment at hand. In this case, the object of the moment at hand is to breathe with all of your being. Become the breath entering your nostrils, traveling down the passageway of your lungs, and diving into the depth of your diaphragm.

When you feel that you have entered a state of total peace, relaxation, and complete consciousness of breath, imagine the most beautiful orange-gold color you can think of. Think of the deep tangerine fire of sunset flung like billowing silk across the heavens. Imagine a tangerine orchard glowing in afternoon light. Feel the glowing orange fruit in your mind. Taste the sweet sun-filled golden nectar; smell the citrus as you envision bruising the warm peel with your fingers. Visualize the topaz dance of fire in the hearth. Think of the wavering flames and gleaming coals beneath the singing, burning wood. Totally immerse your mind and thoughts in the hues of orange-gold while you breathe deeply, thoroughly, almost sensually. Now imagine this beautiful tangerine-gold within your solar plexus, beneath the breastbone. See it as a glimmer that evolves into a blazing explosion of orange light beaming outward from your body. Feel bathed in this sunset-hued brilliance while you continue to breathe as deeply as possible. Allow yourself to pretend to actually become the breath and the light, the orange fire and intake of air.

After a while, you will actually feel a distinct energy or power in the solar plexus area. You may feel a burst of exhilaration, warmth, tingling, or expansion as the center is stimulated. Do not rush to get to this point. Enjoy taking a mental journey into this color energy.

If you experience chills, rapid heartbeat, or dizziness, continue to breathe and visualize. You may feel a tingling sensation throughout your body, drumming in your ears, and spinning in your head. These and any other sensations indicate that you are experiencing a change in consciousness necessary for projection. Many times I've reached this point, knew that projection was soon possible and, out of sheer excitement, broke the entire concentration and lost momentum. So when you reach this stage, work through it and move with the sensations without thought and anticipation. If you get off track, focus on the color and your breathing until you again reach this point. However, if you find yourself getting back on track after four or five attempts, slowly ease back into normal consciousness and try again another day. When pursued more than five times, this technique can leave you feeling very drained, nervous, and even nauseated.

Soon after you experience the above mentioned sensations of consciousness expansion, you should notice a dramatic feeling within your body. You may feel feather-light, completely numb all over, or extremely heavy and weighted to the bed, chair, or floor. An intense, thrilling spinning sensation usually follows. If you have reached a complete change of consciousness, you will leave your body immediately at this point or soon after. You may hear a popping sound, like a cork being removed from a bottle, at the moment your soul body separates from the physical. You may project with force quickly or you may gradually drift outward through your solar plexus area.

When you experience projection, avoid feeling elation or similar emotion until you are out of your body long enough to get used to it. Letting out a "Yahoo! I did it!" even in your mind can suck you right back into your body, so keep a lid on your joy for a little while!

If you are successful leaving the body this way, you may see your silver cord. As stated earlier, you do not *have* to see this rope of energy. However, many people who leave the body through the solar plexus gateway often are the ones who do see it.

After the first few times of leaving the body this way, you may feel dizzy or have a headache or queasy stomach, but after you've practiced this technique further, these sensations should disappear. If not, try another technique if you really feel discomfort.

The Heart Center Technique

The heart center technique is the technique I most often use myself. It is an easy as well as beautiful way of leaving the body. Once I discovered the heart center gateway, I wondered how I ever settled for any other technique.

The heart center, nestled approximately an inch above the breastbone toward the chest, cradles the divine spark of God energy each of us is born with. It is the dwelling place of the soul and the harbor of all elevated emotion such as compassion, unconditional love, and inspiration. Due to the nature of this center, leaving the body through the gateway of the heart can bring you into oneness with the Infinite, which begets extraordinarily beautiful soul journeys.

During times of emotional stress such as grief, longing, anger, or fear, the heart center or chakra can become almost unresponsive. If you are going through such a period, you may wish to work through your feelings before attempting this technique in order to be successful. Even if you do not fully resolve a festering issue, simply spending time with a pet or a loved one can stimulate the heart center with positive energy so this technique can be used. Walking through nature or engaging in creative expression or play can also stimulate this center, like fresh rain into a stagnant pond.

To use the heart center technique, recline on a bed or on a floor surface that is not too hard. You can attempt projection while sitting in a chair, but I find that complete relaxation with the body in a straight line prompts better success rates while using this technique.

To begin, place your power hand (the hand you write with) over the area between your breastbone and where you feel your heartbeat. Take the time to feel your heartbeat beneath your fingertips. As you feel the silent, incessant drumming, think of someone you love, a beautiful memory, or your love for Deity. If you have a favorite childhood memory, remember it in detail. If any memory is your object of focus, recall it with feeling. Return to that distant day and relive each moment that brings you warmth and joy. If you choose to think about someone you love, remember the person's laughter, smile, or voice. If you focus on a lover or spouse, remember his or her eyes lit with sunlight, a whispered touch, or a dissolving embrace. If you think of your longing and reverence for a Higher Power, remember that the glory of this Ultimate Deity resides within the center your hand is resting on. Feel the invisible thread of light that connects you to this power like glimmering gossamer.

Once you feel submerged in your object of focus, begin to breathe deeply and evenly for a few long moments. Feel the breath reach all the way into your diaphragm, filling you with serenity and warmth. Feel your thoughts of Deity, a lover, or a past memory enter your body through your breath. Pretend you are not breathing air but the love that occupies your thoughts. If you have difficulty visualizing this, remember the smell of that lost day in your memory, the smell of your lover's clothes, or the smell of a house of worship, such as an incense-sweetened ashram or a vacant candlelit church.

When you feel that your mind and breathing are somewhat entwined (the more your thoughts and feelings are united, the better), think of the most beautiful rose color you have ever seen. Think of blushing, light-infused clouds hovering in an illumined dawn. Imagine deep pink roses lit with sun, undressing their glowing petals in a gust of morning wind. Feel the flowers' silken clusters between your fingers. In your mind's eye, smell the fragrance of these glowing roses that resemble wine and rain. Envision rose-colored glasses overflowing with sunlight on a windowsill. Completely drench your mind with rose pink until all other thoughts are eclipsed by its fire. Allow the memory, the lover, the Higher Power to dissolve in the color of rose. Imagine this color in the palm of your hand that is resting on your chest. Visualize its pink fire blazing like a star and penetrating your heart. Continue to imagine this transference of light energy until you feel a warmth in your heart center. This warmth will probably progress into a sensation of expansion, as if suddenly a door in your heart has flung open widely and your breathing feels weightless, even exhilarated. Once you reach this point, drop your power hand to your side and surrender entirely to the new sensations.

Now focus your mind on three things only:

- Your breathing

- The bed or floor against your back

- The feeling in your heart center

Focus only on these three things. If other thoughts interfere, allow them to pass and strive to channel all of your concentration into the above three objects of focus. Once you do this, drop one of the three. Now forget your breathing and only think of the bed or floor against your back and the feeling in your heart center. Again, focus only on these two things.

Now, drop another object of focus, the bed or floor against your back, and concentrate only on the feeling in your heart. If you get off track, again think of two things. Once you are able to singularly focus on the feeling in your heart, you should feel inseparable from the heart center itself. You should experience a loss of self and profound communion with the present moment, the consciousness of now. You ARE the heart center. You ARE love. You ARE the fire of the rose, the energy, the power.

If you reach this blissful meditative state and your consciousness is thus expanded into the now, you will leave your body effortlessly through the heart chakra, like a leaf on the wind. The beauty of releasing the physical this way can never be described, only experienced. No matter how many times you must practice this to finally succeed, the results are worth it! Even if you do not experience a successful projection, when done regularly this meditation can have a profound effect on your psychic ability and spiritual evolvement.

The Crown Center Technique (The Mystic's Gateway)

Those who have highly developed spiritual and psychic abilities project through the crown center or chakra at the top of the head. Though this technique can be learned, the process should never be hurried. If it comes naturally, it is safe to pursue; however, there are some precautions for those who are just learning this advanced technique.

The crown chakra, which resides at the rim of the skull, is a powerhouse of soul energy. It is the center that, when stimulated by meditation and spiritual discipline, provokes cosmic consciousness, visions, mystical experiences, and self-knowledge. This center is the mystic's gateway into other worlds. But those who open the crown center too quickly can become spiritually burnt out. Tapping into the tremendous energy of the crown chakra before one is ready to handle it can have an adverse effect on the nervous system of the individual. If you are a beginner or if you are psychically ultrasensitive but not yet proficient, I advise you to go slowly with this technique. As a daily or weekly meditation, the technique itself is excellent for stimulating the crown center, but this work should be balanced with plenty of everyday activities that give you a good sense of grounding. While you are practicing this technique, it is especially important to exercise daily, remain mentally active, and get plenty of sleep and good food.

On the other hand, if you are already developed psychically and spiritually, this technique is ideal for you if you haven't yet succeeded at it naturally. If you have regular mystical experiences, have a good degree of psychic ability, communicate with the spirit world through mediumship, telepathy, or soul travel, experience moments, days, or weeks of profound and undiluted oneness with the universal energies, or have the gift of true healing, then your crown chakra is very much stimulated and open. However, the intensity of this energy center can at times be too much, even for the advanced spiritual seeker, so go by your natural responses. If you find yourself feeling too spaced out, nervous, or overly sensitive to the vibrations of those around you, give yourself time to recharge by using other techniques of projection. Once you feel balanced again, then continue with the crown center technique.

To begin, choose a firm bed or comfortable floor surface on which to recline. Be sure your spine is straight and that your neck is supported with a soft pillow that is not too high. Healthy nerve impulse function is vital for the Kundalini energy to travel up the spine from the genital region to the crown chakra at the rim of the head. Once this Kundalini power reaches the crown center, projection through this gateway and cosmic consciousness will automatically follow.

Breathe slowly and deeply as your body relaxes and melts into the bed or floor. Feel the breath reach your diaphragm. Do this for at least eight minutes, so the oxygen reaches the brain fully. Once you have a feeling of clarity in your head and calmness in your entire body, imagine a prismatic, multicolored ribbon of fire traveling serpent-like from your coccyx to the top of your head. As this rainbow light travels through the pathway of your body, see it illuminating each area as it ascends toward your head. Continue to breathe evenly and deeply. Vividly envision the fire uncoiling and yourself ablaze with breathtakingly beautiful light, reflecting every color of the spectrum. See the ruby and the scarlet flame, the shimmer of spring green, the glimmer of golden yellow, the quiet fire of violet, and the blaze of fuchsia. Feel ignited from head to toe with rainbow light. In your mind's eye, see the prismatic ribbon of energy reaching the top of your head. When this reaches the crown, imagine the spectrum of color exploding into a blinding eruption of silver-white light that sends sparks away from you like shooting stars.

Once you have been visualizing this with feeling for a certain period of time (it varies with each individual), you may feel a coldness along the length of your body when you inhale, as if you have just taken a menthol lozenge. You may also hear the buzzing of bees, the sound of breaking surf, rushing winds, music with exquisite harmony, or any other sound signaling that your consciousness is moving away from the physical plane.

If your consciousness has expanded fully enough and your crown center has been stimulated, you will leave your body through the top of your head. You may hear a popping sound or you may hear a sound that resembles a rush of storm wind. If you do project, you will probably feel as if you've been ejected. After practice, you will be able to control this and just drift out like a buoyant balloon.

This technique may take more time to master if it doesn't work for the individual naturally, but it is well worth pursuing. It is a sure technique that can catalyze extensive journeys to finer inner planes and hard-to-reach locations, such as the Akashic Records (see Chapter 5) and other spiritual libraries.

The Circular Breathing Technique

The circular breathing technique enables you to reach a profound depth in meditation. Even if you do not wish to strive for projection this way, it is a wonderful meditation that you can use as often as you wish and still continue to experience level upon level of awareness. Try it when you feel stressed, upset, or tired. This meditation has even replaced sleep for me when I needed a rejuvenator.

To begin, recline or sit with your back comfortably supported. For this technique I prefer to sit because the benefit from breathing can be fully reaped with a straight spine. If you practice yoga and you are accustomed to sitting in meditation for long periods without back support, you may prefer to use this technique. However, if you are one of the many people who have found meditation to be unpleasant because of the discomfort felt while sitting without back support, I suggest you sit in a chair or lean against a wall while using this technique. Yes, I know that it is part of the yogic discipline to overcome the nagging little aches and pains of the physical body but, if you find that physical discomfort is preventing you from benefiting from meditation, by all means do it the easy way. Having had back problems all of my life, meditation didn't become useable or enjoyable until I leaned against a support.

Whether you choose to sit or recline, take a few moments to center yourself. Imagine that you are a balloon that has just been severed from all of the distractions of daily living. Mentally cut yourself off from the outside world and take time to be. Drift in the heaven of your own calmness.

Once you feel calm, begin breathing slowly and deeply but not so deeply that it is an effort. Get to know the process of breathing that we take for granted. Enjoy it, feel it, know each inhalation and exhalation as a part of your body. As you do this, become aware of the air moving beyond the lungs and into your diaphragm. You will know that the air has been inhaled as deeply as possible when you feel a little tug in your stomach, as if you've just stepped onto a spinning merry-go-round.

Breathe, taking the air into the nostrils, the lungs, the diaphragm, and then hold it for three to four long seconds until you feel the air depressing even further into your diaphragm. After the three or four seconds, gradually exhale, allowing the breath to be released with complete relaxation and fluidity. After five minutes or so of inhaling, holding the breath for a few long seconds and then exhaling will give you the profound sensation that your breath is making an invisible circular pathway.

You will notice your head and sinuses feel clearer as well as a wonderful sensation of lightness in the chest, as if you've just taken a breath of crisp winter air. When you reach this point, you will automatically begin to breathe deeper and slower, taking more time between breaths. Continue to go into this pattern of breathing. Thoughts will dissolve totally into the moment at hand and your mind will feel like a shaded, unrippled pond.

As you continue, you will find that your breathing becomes very slow, very deep, and you are inhaling almost half as much as you ordinarily would. This can feel a little scary, but it is the telltale sign that you are entering a very deep state of meditation. If you practice this daily and allow your entire body and consciousness to dissolve into this state, you will leave your body without effort. If and when you project this way, you will most likely exit through the top of your head via the crown center or chakra. Most yogis leave the body while they are in this state. Aside from projection, after practice, you will be able to view inner planes, experience spiritual rapture, or even taste, hear, and smell many extraordinary things beyond physical perception. The only key is to practice this daily and not hold back when your breathing really slows down and you feel like it could be your last breath. Don't worry—this is completely safe and actually very healing to the nervous system and vital organs.

The Shaman Technique

The shaman technique borrows the use of drumming, dancing, and working with power animals to induce an ecstatic state conducive to astral projection as well as mind travel or remote viewing (the ability to observe distant places and people without actually leaving the body).

This technique is ideal for anyone with an abundance of physical energy who uses dance and movement as a tool for consciousness expansion, or who is exceptionally linked to nature, sound, or tribal cultures.

Personally, I have been very successful with this technique when I used it at the time of sundown. Though any time can be chosen, the best time to use this technique would be at sunrise, noon, sunset, or during the rise of the full moon.

To use the shaman technique, choose an uncluttered and ample room or a private and safe outdoor location. If you choose a room indoors, be sure the floor is cleared of anything you can accidentally step on or bump into. If you choose your site out of doors, be sure you are completely private, safe, and not in danger when the temperature drops or soars or when the tide comes in.

You will need the following:

- Cassette or CD player (battery operated if you are out of doors)

- Music with genuine percussion rhythm (Native American, African, or East Indian Ragas—avoid synthesized percussion; taped live percussion is ideal)

- Incense and incense burner/holder (sticks, cones, or loose variety made of only 100% natural ingredients such as pine, cedar, lavender, myrrh, or sandalwood)

- Candles, saucers, and lighter/matches (use votive or tea light candles with heat-proof saucers or dishes)

- Drum, rattles, rainstick, or tambourine

- A sage wand or bundle of dried lavender stems for smudging

- An abundant amount of one of the following: Dried sage, fresh or dried rose petals, dried yarrow flowers, dried or fresh cedar needles or branches, fresh flowers

Be sure you have all of the above items before you go to your chosen location if it is out of doors or indoors. Even if a needed item is in another room, it will break up the continuity of the ritual or technique if you have to get up to get it. Also before beginning, inspect the area if you are outside. Be sure you are away from tree stumps, rocks, or branches you can later trip over while dancing.

Dress in comfortable clothing or go skyclad if you have your privacy and feel inclined to do so. Feel free to dress in ritual garb as long as your outfit does not hinder your movements or invite injury, such as swinging necklaces, long hems, hair decorations, et cetera. You may want to wear a natural lightweight necklace or crown made of autumn leaves, fresh and pliant willow branches, daisies, or grasses to attune your energies with the earth's vibration. Lastly, go barefoot unless you are at an outdoor location that is pebbly or rocky.

To begin, locate the sun's (or moon's) location according to the time of day (or night). Find the approximate direction of east, west, south, and north. If you are a perfectionist, you may wish to bring a compass with you for accuracy.

Once you find the eastern point, light your sage wand or lavender bundle and allow it to cultivate a good, fragrant smoke that will not die out before you want it to. Be sure all of your needed items are near, for you will be drawing a circle with the wand to enclose yourself within it for psychic protection.

As the smoke is rising from your wand, face the east and begin walking slowly in a clockwise direction. Create an imaginary circle large enough for you to dance and drum within, consciously connecting east to south, south to west, and west to north by using the smoking wand as a pointer.

Once you reach the point where you began the circle, walk around two more times, continuing to use the sage or lavender bundle as your guide. When you complete the circle the third time, move within the circle and wave the fragrant smoke throughout the interior of your psychic sphere. Imagine a ring of white fire blazing around you, encircling you in a protective bubble of power.

If your wand doesn't naturally die out, rub it against the ground if you are outside. If you are inside, jab the ends against one of the saucers you placed nearby 'for a candle. Proceed then by lighting your choice of incense and placing the burner or holder in the eastern corner of your psychic circle. Place a lit candle also in the eastern corner as well as each of the remaining three directions. As you place a candle in the corner of each direction, pause a moment to honor the corresponding element. As you face east, honor air. As you face south, honor fire. As you face west, honor water. And as you face north, honor earth.

Then take either sea salt (use only if you are out of doors), rose petals, yarrow flowers, cedar branches or needles, or fresh flowers and connect the four corners of your circle by strewing the herbs, flowers, or salt. (After the ritual, these substances can easily be swept or vacuumed up if you are indoors.) Don't worry if you do not make a perfect circle with the natural materials. You simply want the physical, visible circle to mirror the original etheric circle.

Put your music on at a volume that is comfortable but stimulating and stand in the middle of the circle. Smell the perfume of the incense while thinking about the abundant beauty of the earth. Listen to the percussion and think about your own powerful life force drumming within your heartbeat and blood flow. Extend your arms away from your sides. Close your eyes and ask the Ultimate Deity to guide you on your journey. Feel free to address this power in the Native American tradition as "Great Spirit."

Once you feel peaceful within the circle, and the candles are dancing with light and the incense is releasing its fragrant soul, begin drumming or shaking your chosen percussion instrument to the beat of the music. Make it your offering to the Invisibles, who tend to all of the growing things on our planet. Think of an animal you feel akin to. Feel love for this wild creature who silently mirrors your own wild and pristine spirit.

Begin to move your body as you drum or shake, becoming an instrument also. Dance, leap, bend, skip, crouch, breathe deeply, losing yourself within sound. If you are outside, revel in the embrace of Mother Nature and all of her sights, sounds, and smells. If you are indoors, imagine being in the heart of the wilderness. Wherever you are, allow the earth's power to intoxicate your entire being. As you drum, think of unbridled surf collapsing against ancient rocky coasts. As you dance, think of October leaves soaring in autumn wind like a flock of golden birds. Allow any instinctual sound to come out. Yelp, howl, sigh, sing, chant, or even growl if you feel like it. Reclaim the wild spirit within. Don't allow self-consciousness to bind you in any way. Ecstasy only blesses those who experience the moment without self-awareness. To achieve such a state is crucial for projection or visions.

Place the instrument in a safe corner of the circle and continue to dance. Lose yourself entirely to the rapture of movement. Dance for all the powers that be. Then begin spinning in clockwise direction until you become very dizzy. When you feel as if you cannot take the dizziness any longer, lie down on your back with your eyes closed. Dissolve into the sensations of the moment. Surrender totally to the spinning inside your head and the beating of your heart.

If you completely surrender to the moment, you will leave your body with unanticipated joy and speed. It may take time for you to reach an ecstatic state, but keep practicing this technique. The way of the shaman can be a beautiful path.

Even if you do not technically project your soul body, you may indeed project your consciousness. If you project only your consciousness, you will see visions or mental pictures that resemble dreaming. This is a powerful aspect of the shamanic experience and can be a forerunner of soul travel. Nevertheless, it is an important and powerful ability by itself. Through consciousness projection, you can observe any plane of being, any person, place, or thing. It can be an implement for time travel, past life regression, viewing future events, recalling soul journeys of the dream state, solving riddles of the subconscious, and even for experiencing the consciousness of animals or plants.

The Consciousness Projection Technique (Remote Viewing)

After contacting my soul guide during my teen years, I learned how to observe distant places with her assistance. Eventually the observations became so incredibly close at hand that I was often in two places at one time. I could feel the morning rain in Santa Monica, California. I could smell bread baking in a small New England café. I could touch my father standing in a garage a mile away, yet I felt no distinct separation from my physical body. I didn't see the famous silver cord. I could also be aware of any intrusion or distraction in my immediate environment. It was like having three-dimensional sight while viewing a riveting movie in a private theater. This was my initiation into the world of soul projection.

One day, with startling joy, I realized I was at the location I was viewing. I could drift, walk through walls, and even dance like a monkey around someone who couldn't see or hear me. In essence, I first projected my mind or consciousness to the distant place, then donned a finer body to travel with. This was a completely natural process, for I was unaware that I had even done it. Though projecting this way came fairly easy, it took me years to understand its nature. The only drawback to accomplishing projection with this technique is that during periods of physical or mental fatigue it is very difficult to do. Since projecting the mind takes incredible energy as it is, it proves to be exhausting to fully leave the body when you are tired. For reference, you may wish to read *The Spiral Dance: A Re-*

birth of the Ancient Religion of the Great Goddess by Starhawk. She briefly discusses the nature of consciousness projection in the "Trance" chapter.

Practicing the consciousness projection technique can sharpen your psychic skills. Until distant places can be observed with total clarity, do not worry about donning a form to travel with. It will happen so naturally and gradually that you will hardly notice the transition, save for your enthusiasm.

To practice remote viewing or projecting your consciousness, choose a quiet spot to sit or recline. Morning hours are especially conducive for success. If you can, make time before getting out of bed to practice this technique.

Relax your breathing as well as your muscles. Imagine you are floating on your back in sunlit aquamarine water. Pretend you are drifting, feeling the shimmering waters supporting you. Once you feel serene in body and mind, focus on a place you would like to visit, perhaps a favorite location or somewhere you've never been. For example, you may concentrate on your hometown or a major city. Repeat in your mind the name of the place over and over. Don't try to see images. Totally relax as you think of the name of the location.

Do this until you begin to see pictures or hear sounds in your mind. They may appear very hazy at first, or they may come in vivid flashes like a slide show. Some people have to practice this technique for a very long time before they see images, while others view scenes during the first attempt. In either case, never dismiss your impressions as subconscious leftovers! And also a word of advice: Don't allow anyone to set a time and date with you to partake in your remote viewing. For example, don't attempt to see what your brother is doing at a certain time on a certain day and then try to prove it. The pressure of performing or achieving accuracy is enough to dull your ability or even block it entirely. Instead, test your accuracy by observing the weather at a particular location.

After viewing, check the weather service. If you see names of towns or stores, you may wish to check maps and travel guides as well. But don't get discouraged if you can't find a town or establishment. Travel guides cannot list every store, restaurant, and attraction of any given area, and maps can be outdated. Perhaps the location is in a different state than you believed it to be. Or, less likely but very possibly, you traveled back into time or into the future of that place and viewed what is no longer there or not yet manifested! So, go easy on yourself, and try to understand the nature of mind travel.

How to Time Travel. Traveling back into the past or to the future via consciousness projection can be an exciting tool. However, sometimes we may see future events that never manifest. This is due to the fact that every person on this planet has free will. The future, no matter how fixed in probability, is subject to change because of free will. This is why so many genuine and accurate psychics can be wrong. The energy form of the possibility is already within the astral world, the birthplace of all manifested reality. However, due to our thoughts and actions within the physical world, this energy form can be dissolved or altered at any moment before it makes its way into the physical realm.

By the same token, sometimes we view past events that we cannot find in history books. This is simply because no one, anywhere, knows every detail of everything that has ever happened. So, trust your experiences, no matter what. If you are honestly certain that you viewed something or someone beyond your own conjuring, then, in all probability, you did.

Time travel is simple once you learn remote viewing. To view your past lives, completely relax. Think about a place you went to or an incident that transpired a year ago. Recall as many details as you can. Then remember something from five years ago, ten years ago, or twenty years ago. Be sure to pause long enough to remember the memory vividly. Eventually, recall years in your childhood until you run out of conscious memories.

When you reach this point, breathe deeply three times. On the third inhalation, say aloud or mentally, "Before this life." These three simple words are enough to continue the retrieval of memories that you've begun with memories of your current life. Continue to say these words over and over until you begin to feel sensations or see images. You will know when and if you begin to remember past existences.

Once you remember a distant time, place, or incident, hold the memory. Use all of your senses. See details. Hear sounds. Feel sensations. The process of becoming absorbed into the memory is very much like what happens when you become immersed in a film. An hour goes by and then you realize that for those sixty minutes you were not experiencing the character's circumstances but sitting comfortably in a chair with the cat in your lap. Allow the images or sensations to eclipse your current experience. When you become part of the image you remember through your senses, which brings your entire consciousness back into time. No matter how many times you have to practice this, eventually you will be successful. And when you are, you will be in another body, in another time and place. At first it will feel as if you are watching a very familiar character whom you feel a kinship with. Over a course of minutes, you will then enter your past consciousness and relive portions of that life. Though you will be absorbed in that time, place, and personality, you have the power to return to your current life and mind whenever you wish to. This is the beauty of self-regression. However, when the images fade and you come back, or when you choose to return, be sure to remember things that happened last week or yesterday. Ground yourself once again by fully returning to this life.

If you want to relive incidents in history, simply say aloud or mentally the place or event you wish to witness. For example, say or think "World War I." Or simply think of a year, such as "1544." Repeat the place, event, or year until you begin to see images or feel sensations. The process will be identical to past life retrieval, but you will not don another identity unless you lived during that particular time on this plane. You will not be able to converse with anyone you see or be able to contribute to the outcome of events.

Once you get a taste of time travel, it is very easy to become obsessed with the possibility of reliving lives and events. If you experience this, get what you can out of your newfound ability and interest, then try to put it all in perspective. When all is said and done, the life we are living now is the most important one. We aren't just killing time until we come back around again with a more perfected body and bank account. We cannot change the past or plan a future life, but we can find our purpose in this present consciousness. Have fun, but don't take time travel too seriously, because the most beautiful experiences are the ones we have yet to see in this body, this time, this place.

Time travel and self-regression can also be applied when you wish to re-experience or remember nocturnal out-of-body journeys that are often beyond remembrance in the busy routine of daily living. This will be discussed below, following the twilight technique.

The Twilight Technique

The twilight technique is for anyone who finds it difficult to project during full waking consciousness. It is also more convenient for those who can't find the time to practice the other techniques. However, clarity may suffer, and it is possible that the individual may fall asleep only to awaken with little memory (if any) of the journey.

The twilight technique is designed for projection just prior to sleep. This shadowy time before sleep is the time when the mind releases the day's events, leaving space for psychic impressions, visions, insights, and the like. It is the time between the waking and dream state, an inviolate moment when the door between worlds is left ajar.

Most people can recall times when they just drifted off to sleep only to be suddenly awakened by jerking motions of the body. To the average person, being startled from sleep this way is simply due to contracting muscles that are finally being relaxed after a hectic day. On the other hand, more often than not, this occurs when the soul body begins to separate from the physical and, due to any number of reasons, gets pulled back.

To use the twilight technique before a night's sleep or even an afternoon nap, lie down on your back. Deep breathe until your muscles relax, and allow the day's events to dissolve as you focus solely on your projection goal. You can use a mental affirmation, such as "I'm leaving my physical body" or "I'm going to so-and-so place." Say the affirmation in your mind with feeling and faith. Visualize drifting out of your body and flying. Envision the place where you want to go.

Focus on your goal and affirmation without too much effort. Sometimes affirmations and visualizations can keep the conscious mind too alert to reach the twilight state, where you feel yourself submerging into light sleep. So, concentrate with ease, rather than making it like a mental exercise. Daydream.

When you feel yourself going into light sleep, it is then possible that you will naturally project. Many, many people fall asleep attempting this technique. Don't get discouraged if you are one of the majority. It takes practice to seize that precise moment without sleep overwhelming you. If your intent is strong and focused, with time, you will be successful. But even if sleep follows, you will most probably go out of your body in the dream state. It requires effort to consciously remember your journey. Most often you will recall some of the elements in a dream, but the remembrance of the actual soul journey can get interwoven with subconscious symbols. When this happens, you have to pick out the truth from the fantasy. As previously mentioned, self-regression is the only sure way to retrieve every second of your sojourn without having subconscious intrusion.

Self-Regression for Remembering Nocturnal Spirit Journeys. After you have attempted the twilight technique or after a night's sleep, you may wish to regress yourself to remember where your spirit has gone while you slept. After you learn how to do this, you will become so accustomed to knowing what your spirit body does during nocturnal hours that you will eventually have no need to actually regress yourself in the morning. You will then be so in tune with your other self that you will simply remember journeys as if you've taken them physically.

To remember nocturnal journeys, as soon as you awaken in the morning, after a nap, or even in the middle of the night, try to remain in that state between full waking consciousness and sleep. Languish in the dream-like silence, allowing images to pass across the screen of your mind's eye. Out-of-body memories will be clear and repetitive, while other pictures will come and go without returning. Do not try to remember or see. Simply be a bystander. You may remember by feeling. Many times I awaken after sleep and actually feel Paris in my gut or actually smell rain or flowers of a place where I'd gone as I slept. Yes, pay attention to all of your senses. Each sense has a memory bank, like our brain.

Once you feel or see a memory, say to yourself mentally, "I am back there once again. Wherever my spirit has gone, I am there again." At this point, the images will intensify. Repeat those same words over and over until you indeed relive the journey. When you come out of the regression, you may be awed by the time that has gone by. If you want to know how long your nocturnal sojourn was, notice the time when you first see images and when you "come back" from reliving the memory. Count the minutes and you'll have the amount of time. Many times I come out of self-regression and realize two hours have gone by so, if you have a set schedule, be sure to consider this angle for practicality!

All of these techniques may take many hours of practice, but all can be learned. If necessary, allow yourself a lifetime to learn and perfect the art of soul projection as well as anything. An artist as well as a scientist can accomplish great things in the early years, but none can argue that in later years they are still accomplishing great things but for the knowledge of shortcuts, wisdom, and the skill that only comes by doing something often. Love what you are doing or trying to do; the rest will follow. On the other hand, the path of the mystic and the shaman never concludes, in this lifetime or beyond. It is an ongoing lesson in knowing the Divine Self. So, don't get too comfortable in your abilities and successes. The greatest heights to be reached are the ones we have yet to strive for.

Chapter Five

Soaring the Heavens

Exploring

the Invisible

The physical world that penetrates every aspect of our existence is but one minute fragment in the entirety of reality, a single color in the kaleidoscope of being. Just as the view from our kitchen window does not encompass the entire world, our physical eyes cannot perceive the countless layers of realms beyond the five senses.

Upon an uncharted path,
   During an hour's wandering,
   I found the Elysian Fields.
   Unaware of my presence, hidden,
   The Gods drank sunlight and supped on dreams
   Lost by mortal men.
   Long hidden, long I watched them,
   Gods now ignorant of Time and earthly fames
   Steadily burning in the world behind them . . . .

These infinite and invisible worlds are only accessible by traveling in the soul body. It is impossible for any spirit traveler to exhaust all the planes and subplanes that exist, but this knowledge alone is thrilling; the immensity of existence is as awe-inspiring as the invisible worlds themselves.

Unfortunately, you cannot go to the corner market and buy a map of these fantastic realms and arrange a trip with camera and souvenir bag in hand. Many times travelers experience projection to particular realms and places without intention. As stated before, thought is your vehicle. If you have some idea of location, what to expect, and how to use the etheric passageways or tunnels, then you will most likely be able to direct your projection with much more ease, skill, and success.

Here I will discuss in depth the planes I have traveled to, how I got there, the afterlife and visiting loved ones, as well as how to enter the higher, finer spiritual realms via chakra opening and closing and transforming into a light body. Lower worlds and their function and dangers will also be described. Before doing so, I'd like to stress again that your experience may not be identical to mine. Also, the charts I have included of the invisible planes are arranged as I have experienced and understood them.

Using Etheric Passageways

From my knowledge, there are three passageways or tunnels that connect the physical world to the higher and lower realms of existence: the death tunnel, the lower tunnel, and the birth tunnel. These passages are not needed to explore the astral parallels of the earth and the universe, but they do play an important role in travel and exploration of any plane above the earth plane as well as the lower astral (see chart on pages 101-103). However, as you progress in your ability to travel between worlds, you may reach the level of experience and development where you find the use of passageways superfluous. If you refine your spiritual gift to such an extent, you can leave your body and immediately be in such a delicate, fine spiritual realm that you automatically don a light form.

Whether you reach this point or even wish to should not be a concern, because even if you become adept at astral projection, you will probably enjoy traveling through the passageways so much that you will choose to use them.

These etheric tunnels are actually great vortexes of energy that have a powerful magnetic force that propels the soul body forward. Each passage is different in nature, therefore each one gives you a different sensation and experience. You may be wondering, "How do I find them?" Simple. The soul body has a memory of all invisible worlds and how to get there, so all you have to do is think of entering these realms and your spirit will automatically find the appropriate gateway. If you prefer to focus on the passage instead, the result will be the same.

Your next question may be, "Do you travel back to the physical world through the same tunnel also?" Yes, usually, but not always. Sometimes you may just return to your physical body but, if you can, avoid doing so. Until you reach and maintain a shamanic level of soul travel ability, returning suddenly without the use of a gateway can cause you to experience headaches, dizziness, nausea, or nervousness due to the change of vibration. There is also the danger of leaving some of your psychic energy in the astral plane, which can leave you depleted or even exhausted if it is habitual.

The Death Tunnel

The death tunnel is the passage to higher realms beyond the earth plane. Souls fresh from the death experience, as well as living soul travelers, use this gateway. Bosch, the fifteenth-century Dutch painter, was one of the first artists to depict this passageway that so many people describe after near-death experiences.

During the years, the death tunnel has always appeared the same to me. A golden light shines from a distance, but those not experiencing death will not witness the blinding white light so many people report; only during the transition of death is the light of such purity and intensity. Within this tunnel I have also seen pulsing spheres of light, some spinning like flaming wheels while others remain stationary. Among this light energy I have also seen tiny flames of color the size of blinking fireflies. No matter how many times you go through this tunnel, you will be amazed at the breathtaking bursts of colored fire.

I have also seen many spirit forms and faces. While traveling through this vortex, they are so bound on their journey that they seem distant and dispassionate. However, there have been times when I encountered desperate spirits or entities with outstretched arms. If you encounter these energies, continue to travel through the passageway without stopping to be comforting, compassionate, or helpful. It is very much like riding the subway: keep your wits about you and let your head, rather than your heart, guide you safely to your destination. These entities are hungry for your energy and will suck it out from your force field without hesitation.

Your flight through the death tunnel will be one of tremendous speed and exhilaration. Though wild and wonderful, it has taken me years to get accustomed to these wind-swept flights that, at times, make you feel as if you are on a roller coaster right after consuming a double-scoop ice cream cone. Once I learned how to open the first two or even three chakra centers for a grounding effect, I was able to control my own speed and simply enjoy the furious flight. To open your chakras for grounding, after you are out of body but before you go through the tunnel, place both hands over the root chakra (at the base of the spine) and move them in a clockwise direction while visualizing light moving from your fingertips into the chakra. Once you feel a wave of expansion or warmth in the area, the center is open. After you open the root chakra, repeat the same procedure and open the second chakra (located near the navel).

The Lower Tunnel

Many people and occult schools of thought today dismiss the existence of lower worlds, or hell. Many stress that the only hell is the one we create in our own minds out of fear or religious doctrine. Yet others who are near-death survivors report visiting hell worlds.

I was a hell skeptic until my soul guide took me on a journey to the lower astral for the sake of knowledge and experience. Yes, we do attract our fears and expectations, but there are also lower realms that serve as classrooms for the soul in need of this experience. They do not exist for punishment, only learning. These realms are fragments of the spiritual whole that are created and sustained by humanity's fears, negative desires, violence, and pain. I will discuss these realms in as much depth as I can later in this chapter for the sake of information, but I do not advise you to travel within the lower astral for any reason. However, if you do, you should only venture into them with a very powerful, reliable, and protective guide.

There is a separate passageway that leads to the lower astral level. Though after physical death some spirits briefly experience a hell world, they initially cross over to the light realms via the death tunnel first, but there are exceptions. As a soul traveler, if you travel to the lower astral you will journey through a very unpleasant passageway. This tunnel is dark, with a density in vibration that will make you feel as if you are traveling through thick liquid. There is also a sensation of extreme coldness and dampness. Unlike the beautiful light-filled death tunnel, the lower tunnel is polluted with repulsive thought forms the color of muddy green, grayish red, and smoky brown. There are countless beings that urge you onward due to the fact that they are getting vicarious pleasure in your descent and are feeding off of your vitality.

The only way to travel through this tunnel and into the lower astral, if you must, is to first close all chakras except the first, the root chakra. Doing this ensures that your psychic chakras and emotional centers are protected from the overwhelming negativity you will encounter. Again, I must stress the danger of entering these realms and the vital necessity of closing the chakras even when you are with a powerful spiritual guide. To close all the chakras but the root, place both hands over the crown center (at the rim of the skull) and move them in a counterclockwise direction while visualizing light moving from your fingertips into the chakra. When you feel a tightness or retraction in the center, it is closing. Repeat this procedure with each chakra (check the chakra chart on page 10 for review, if necessary) until all centers are closed and protected except the root. IMPORTANT: Always re-open or re-stimulate each chakra you close before returning to the physical body, but wait until you are out of the lower tunnel or planes. If you do not re-open the centers, you are inviting serious damage to your emotional and spiritual well-being. To re-stimulate the chakras, use the technique on pages 98-99.

As a final word, I advise that you read about the lower realms later in this chapter before making any decisions about journeying there.

The Birth Tunnel

The birth tunnel is the passage souls use when reincarnating on the earth plane. This exquisite vortex of energy propels the soul essence toward a new life.

Soul travelers can use this gateway when they wish to experience birth or even remember their own. Being in this passageway makes you realize and remember how happy, even euphoric, we were to experience a physical body. No matter what fate waited for us at the conclusion of this glorious gateway, our joy knew no bounds.

The birth tunnel is filled with beautiful light and shines as if made of sun-reflective gold. This gateway vibrates with even deeper and brighter color bursts than the death tunnel. When traveling through this passage, it is like soaring through sun-penetrated crystal. Your soul body feels as if it absorbs the color, and you feel exhilarated and transformed. Countless specks of metallic gold light resembling gold dust fills the entire gateway, like blowing sand. These little flecks of light are actually souls on their way to a new life.

You can use this tunnel to re-experience your own birth, someone else's, or to simply recharge your spirit with unconditional, undiluted, and ecstatic happiness. After you have seen the golden river of reincarnating souls and heard the faint echoes of laughter and baby cries from the distance, you will never forget that, despite the dark pain of living, it is a privilege to be who we are right here, right now.

Outline of Planes and Subplanes

1. Earth Plane

    A. Astral parallel of earth plane:
        where nature spirits and elementals reside

    B. Astral parallel of universe:
        where planetary rulers and lower
        extraterrestrials reside

    C. Realm of cause and effect:
        where all karmic debts are housed

    D. Lower astral:
        Realms of thought forms; where all negative
        emotions are collected; realms perceived as hell

2. Transition Plane

    A.   Reunion realm:
        where souls fresh from the death experience
        reside temporarily; the meeting place where soul
        guides and loved ones are reunited

    B.   Vibrational healing realm:
        where chakra temples are located; realm of spirit
        physicians; realms of healing and rest for those
        who experience traumatic deaths

    C.   Discarnate realm:
        where souls waiting to incarnate and reincarnate
        receive instruction before physical birth

3. Plane of Creativity

    A.   Sound realms:
        where healing with vibrational and spiritual
        properties of sound and music is practiced

    B.   Creative realms (the Dionysian Ray):
        the birthing place of all artistic work that is of a
        pure emotional nature; realms of intense color,
        beauty, feeling, and inspiration; realms of gods,
        goddesses, and semi-divine beings

4. Plane of Pure Thought

    A.   Higher creativity realm:
        source of all finite and infinite knowledge; birthing
        place of all elevated arts and sciences of intellectual
        or spiritual nature

    B.   Realm of knowledge:
        location of Akashic Records and other spiritual
        libraries, universities, et cetera

5. Plane of Being

    A.   Realms of advanced teachers and souls

    B.   Realms of light energy and light beings

6. Plane of Energy (The Avatar Ray)

    A.   Angelic kingdoms:
        realm of the celestial hierarchy and light gods

B.   Realm of the masters:
where spiritual masters and true saints dwell

C.   Realm of divinity:
where the ultimate god/goddess energy dwells

7.   Plane of the Unknown
Source of All

Earth Plane

Traveling Within the Astral Parallel of the Earth

For the first few times of conscious projection, you will most probably travel to various locations in the physical world. Initially, you
will see the world as you would in your physical body. As you learn
how to use your astral senses, finer elements within the physical
world will also be visible and vivid. Instead of only seeing the red-
wood forests, for example, you will see the innumerable beings and
energy forms that inhabit these natural places. The same for bodies
of water, sunlit clouds, volcanoes and fire sources, and deserts.
These beings are commonly classified as nature spirits, fairies, elementals, and devas. For the sake of our human tendency to label
things, there have been many names and classifications of these
invisible beings but, from my own experience as a soul traveler,
these labels are unimportant because of the indescribable diversity
of these energies. Just as there are millions of life forms discovered
and undiscovered in our natural world, there are infinite races of
beings in the astral kingdoms that parallel the earth plane.

While out of body at a natural location such as a forest, beach,
desert, or mountain, you are able to enter these kingdoms that
have been reduced to the fanciful fluff found in children's tales. No
matter what your perception is of these realms, there will always be
beauty, adventure, and surprises that will catch you off guard. But

after all is said and done, you will have beautiful experiences as long as you enter these kingdoms with pure intention, respect, and a child's curiosity.

Just as nature has many faces and many astral realms, so do the changeable, mysterious, and diverse beings found there. There are energy forms of lower etheric evolvement that resemble web-like thought forms and finer, light-infused energies that mirror the angelic intelligences. There are many beings between these two poles of evolvement, and communication of some form or another with them is indeed possible. Communication can vary from telepathy to projection of auric light to simple exchange of vibrational messages. When you wish to communicate with any being or advertise benevolence, imagine a rose-colored light extending outward from your heart center. This easy visualization immediately sends light energy from this chakra to the astral being. I have used this form of greeting on all planes when I have approached elementals, as well as any other spirit to be found. If the being or energy responds by projecting light from its force field, then communication has begun. If the astral form is evolved enough, telepathy is possible. Sometimes telepathy results in a simple exchange of visual images between the traveler and the spirit, so don't always expect a flurry of mental words. If you are concerned about not being able to learn telepathy, relax. It will happen automatically. In fact, it is virtually an instinct of the soul.

As discussed in Chapter 2, contacting an elemental guide can take you further into these realms, but even if you explore alone, there are wonders to be found. No matter what you see, don't feel that you are experiencing a mental regression. Yes, there are beings that have bodies of energy that have both human and animal characteristics, or even resemble plant life. There are mazes and etheric dwelling places within the earth—shimmering, prismatic cities within clouds and sunset fire; spirit lights blinking like fireflies among trees; faces and dancing forms in fire; and haunting, singing beings beneath waterfall pools and thundering surf. All or some may appear as they have in myth for thousands of years, or they may appear as light. Ultimately, you will find layers of spiritual life that overlap and interact with each other.

Personally, I have many thrilling memories of traveling within the astral parallel of the earth plane. During one memorable journey, I came face to face with a male sea spirit. The haunting beauty of his iridescent face was framed by what appeared to be indigo-black hair. His lower torso was a swirling prism of light energy that resembled the graceful gossamer of a fish tail. With the sensuous yet pure grace of a dancer, he extended transparent, web-like fingers as I followed suit. As soon as we touched our curious palms together, I felt an exhilarating shock of energy flash through my entire soul body. For a few brief moments that seemed eternal, we communed without verbal or even telepathic communication. Our two worlds, so obviously opposite yet infinitely the same, melded with intimate trust that I will never forget. We studied one another through the green, dimly lit undulations of the sea while other etheric forms of light drifted around us. Then, without words or thoughts, he dissolved back into the depths. To this day, I have not forgotten the inviolate significance of feeling on that beautiful face that seemed to emerge from a child's sweet dream.

Though I have not personally encountered a hostile or dangerous being in any of these elemental kingdoms, I advise you to be cautious. Do not pursue any energy that indicates it wishes to be left alone or acts threatening in any way.

Traveling Within the Astral Parallel of the Universe

Just as the earth has an astral parallel of life energy, so do the planets, stars, moons, and suns. Exploring space in its physical form or etheric form can be both exhilarating and terrifying. The first time I projected into space, the silence and feeling of isolation over-whelmed me. However, with the suggestion from a soul guide, when I experienced such uneasiness, I willed myself to the sun. If you run into the same feelings while exploring space, I suggest you do the same. Once you see the power and unspeakable beauty of the sun's pulsating fire, all anxiety should vanish. There are no words that could possibly describe this cosmic giant, but once you witness its majesty, fear of further space exploration seems to dissolve.

After I saw the sun, I again ventured into the starry blackness, but this time, instead of feeling isolated, I felt one with the entire universe. I listened beyond the silence and heard distant voices of exquisite beauty and harmony. I saw quickly moving forms of silver light dart just beyond my reach and shimmering, angelic beings within the glimmering gases of the stars.

Each heavenly body has an etheric sovereign, just as our planet has a protective mother that governs all physical and astral life forms. These supreme, celestial rulers vary in form, appearance, and nature, but are accessible if you enter their psychic worlds with humility and without selfish motives or power issues. My experience with such beings has been very useful in my own spiritual growth, especially my encounters with the female divinities of Neptune and the earth's moon. Though most are extremely elusive and selective in who they choose to appear to, with patience and respect these kingdoms can not only be explored but their rulers can serve as spiritual teachers as well.

Over a two-month period, I traveled to Neptune and was fortunate to penetrate the etheric kingdom of this beautiful blue planet. Its ruler is a massive female energy draped in cascades of aqua and sapphire blue. She is a loving yet very authoritative being with a gleaming white staff. This being can serve as a powerful teacher in areas of discipline, self-esteem, and courage. Her lessons can be difficult but eventually rewarding. Silver-white lightships are numerous within her astral realm, as well as strange but beautiful energies that seem to be submissive to her. Like the astral kingdoms of other planets, Neptune houses many realms within realms. Countless glimmering stairways create labyrinths of light, and blue and lavender mists curtain most of the areas I explored.

Unlike Neptune and its ruler, the astral energy of the moon is divided into two very distinct etheric environments. The bright, reflective side of the moon is very delicate in nature and resembles a quiet summer garden at night. Here I found a silver-blue world of painfully beautiful and fragrant flowers; hidden shadowy pools of mirrored water; soft, shining showers of rain; and a mesmerizing ruler of female energy. The Queen of the moon is the most elusive of the planetary and universal beings and, once looked upon, can never be forgotten. I remember her as having a long, lithe form, finely sculpted features with upturned, elongated eyes, and a glistening frame of silver hair that falls and shines like a moonlit waterfall. Her entire body was enshrouded in sparkling white mists. In the brief moments of being near her presence, I felt healed and completely spellbound by spiritual love. The purity of this being and the bright side of the moon is indescribable. If you choose to explore space, I advise you to visit the moon, but be patient in finding its Lady.

On the other hand, the dark side of the moon can be very frightening. The astral world of this area is scarred with black jagged cliffs, dark recesses, and unpleasant beings with black robes, ashen faces, and devilish natures. I did not explore this half of the moon's kingdom out of pure uneasiness but, if you have a strong sense of curiosity and a strong auric shield, you may wish to pursue this area in depth.

Again, I advise caution, common sense, and wisdom to know when not to pursue a being. Overall, projecting into space can teach you many things and prepare you for the beauty and uniqueness of the spiritual realms beyond the earth and the galaxies.

Lower Astral Planes

It would be logical to think that the lower astral or hell worlds would be lower in vibration than the earth but, in reality, the earth— being physical and dense—is the lowest in vibratory rate. We can see, hear, taste, smell, and touch the earth with our five physical senses while the lower astral is only tangible to the soul body.

These lower realms have been literally created by humankind's negative thoughts, emotions, and actions, and are constructed of resulting thought forms. Like the higher realms, the lower astral worlds are necessary in the spiritual scheme of things, but exploring them for the fun of it is very dangerous. They are intended for education for any soul who needs it after the transition of death; they are not useful on any level to a soul traveler.

Since like attracts like, vibrations are no exception. When a soul passes through the doors of death, after the initial transition, it then immediately goes to a plane of like vibration. The sum of all actions, experiences, and thoughts of a particular life determines a soul's level of vibrational energy. This means that a person of great intellect or art would naturally find himself within the higher spiritual realms where beauty, color, and sound dominate with ecstatic intensity. This also means that if a person experienced great emotional or mental pain for most of his physical life, he may find himself in one of the lower realms not because he was ignorant or spiritually unevolved but because he is vibrationally akin to the subworlds due to the great thought forms that were created from the pain. Another possible case would be someone who inflicted great physical or emotional suffering on other people. His vibration would be in tune with a lower world if he were a murderer, for example, but he would find himself there for the sake of experiencing personally what was committed.

Just because these worlds are illusion and are part of the cosmic balance does not mean that evil does not exist. We have all heard that evil is a state of mind, a concept especially of modern theology, and a preconceived notion in the category of demons, goblins, and monsters under the bed. But from my own experience of these realms, there is no doubt in my mind or spirit that, within human potential, evil is possible, real, and threatening to the spiritual aspirant. Beyond religious dogma, melodramatics, and our worldly conceptions of it, evil is a reality and has a place in the lower astral realm.

I sincerely hope that you will not travel within these realms, but if you do, please do so under the direction of a powerful and protective guide or guides. Never do so when you are emotional, depressed, angry, suicidal, sexual, fearful, physically ill, or dealing with an addiction (yours or anyone else's). I say this with such precaution because the negativity of these worlds can never be imagined, much less prepared for. The negativity, thought forms, and entities are made of what your spirit is made of: vibrational matter. This means that you can absorb anything you come in contact with like a sponge, with the speed and suction of a vacuum. In simple and direct terms, you can bring back half of hell with you and have a snowball's chance of getting rid of your newfound company.

For the sake of information, here is a brief list of the major lower planes. There are countless subplanes just like the higher realms, so it is impossible to know all of them, much less list them all.

Blueprint of the Earth. This first lower plane holds all pain and suffering experienced on earth. The landscape vividly resembles the earth's inner chambers. This plane is very dark, primitive, and agonizing in feeling. Imagine the worst heartbreak you have ever endured or the most acute physical agony you have ever felt, then multiply that a hundred times with the sensation of being buried alive. That is what this plane feels like.

Many people who have suffered mentally, emotionally, and physically during their lifetime and cannot raise their vibration due to heavy thought form build-up go briefly to this realm until the negative energy can be transformed into more positive energy. This process can only be understood after we experience death.

Plane of Violence. This second plane of the lower astral is the temporary dwelling place of murderers, those who have committed violent crimes and acts, and those who have died by violent suicide. It is interesting to note that the act of suicide itself does not bring one here, but the *way* one chooses to end one's life.

The expression to "burn in hell" probably sprang from some unconscious knowledge of this realm. The landscape is unbearably hot, arid, and boiling with rivers of scarlet energy resembling fire and volcanic lava. Energies resembling demons and entities with horrific deformities dominate this plane. Black thought forms and frightening entities crowd the numerous caverns and corridors of this plane. Rage, fear, and pain are so thick, you feel as though you are paralyzed beneath a fallen tree. When I passed through this realm, I remember seeing unspeakable murders being committed in my mind's eye. Apparently, I had psychically peered into the memories of the thought forms. Of all of the realms of the underworld, this one, in my opinion, is the most evil and frightening.

Plane of Deviance. The third plane of the lower astral is temporary public housing for all rapists, molesters, and anyone who had an abundance of negative sexual energy. Only those who have hurt other people or themselves with violent lust go here—this does not include people who love sex or who are not heterosexual.

All sexual demons, including the incubus and succubus, reside here and are very dangerous. Spirits of this plane feed off of the negative sexual energy of the living as well as the unresolved deceased. During my journey to this realm, I witnessed spirits in violent orgasmic ecstasy absorbing smoke-colored sexual energy from an unknown source.

There were so many of these insatiable, throbbing entities that it was very difficult to travel through this plane. The landscape of this realm is dark and jagged with a blackish-crimson haze resembling thick fog. Tar-like substances drip into swirling, foul-smelling pools. Overall, the most noticeable thing, other than the crowd of lustful spirits, is the odor of uncleanliness.

Plane of Fear. This plane is the place where all fears are manifested. It is indescribably frigid and is basically a wasteland of iced-over trees that reach into the opaque grayness like bony arms. The feeling of isolation cannot be explained, nor can the desolation.

I saw no human-like spirits, only drifting mists of aimless thought forms. Every fear I ever knew flooded my brain, and it took every ounce of strength to fight paralysis. For me, this realm was the most unbearable.

Plane of Dark Forces. This final major plane is a realm of concentrated negative energy, a plane of dark sorcery and black practitioners. The thought forms and powerful evil of this world are overwhelming. The countless beings here can aptly be called hell's angels. Their ugliness, diversity, and dark wings of energy cannot be imagined.

There is a dreadfully massive being, beast-like in nature and appearance, that seems to govern this plane. Perhaps this is the source of the concept of the devil.

Anyone who inflicted harm, pain, or loss upon others via the Black Occult Arts comes here temporarily.

All of these realms serve as a "lower university" for those in need of it. They are only a small portion of the whole and should not be studied, analyzed, or explored. The higher realms are much more fascinating, spellbinding, beneficial, and unforgettable, so let's move on to more positive things!

Transitional Plane

The transitional plane can be considered the second plane, the earth plane being the first. Within this plane there is a reunion realm, where souls fresh from the death experience reside temporarily. There, a soul is reunited with loved ones and guiding spirits before moving on.

A few hours after my father passed on, I pushed away my grief and left my body to find him. It was within the reunion realm where I found him. I will never forget traveling through beautiful purple mist to a place where many bridges connected portions of the landscape. Beyond it, the plane resembled the most unforgettable places on earth, but vibrated in deeper color intensity. To my surprise, Dad acted as if death was as natural as breathing and nothing significant had happened. Though my heart was brimming with grief, I found great joy knowing that all was well and that he had just begun a very important journey. I knew I couldn't stay long because he had things to do, but it was only the first of countless meetings I would have with him. It has been five years since the night of his passing and, in all honesty, I must say that we know and understand one another more deeply now than when he was alive.

Deceased Loved Ones, the Afterlife, and the Process of Death

Since the event of death takes most souls initially to the transitional plane, this is a good place to discuss visiting loved ones who have passed on. Yes, it is more than possible to have positive, ongoing relationships with the deceased.

Most of us travel to the inner worlds during sleep to visit relatives and friends who have moved on, but rarely do we take the memory of it back with us to waking consciousness unless we net a beautiful and vivid dream from the experience. If you would like to plan a meeting with your loved one, a few hours before you attempt to leave your body, simply ask in prayer to find him or her. Speak to the person; ask him or her to meet you somewhere within the inner planes. Even if you do not meet up the first or even the third time, continue to ask and continue to pursue it. Occasionally, a loved one has reincarnated once again, but this does not necessarily mean that communication is hopeless.

Though the soul essence transfers to another physical body when it reincarnates on the earth plane, fragments of that spirit still exist and can communicate and interact with you. This happened to my father, who was still able to meet his mother after his passing even though she had reincarnated. He spoke of meeting a soul fragment of the identity he knew as his mother and was very pleased. However, when meeting a fragment of a reincarnated soul, it usually is not possible to have an ongoing relationship as you would with a complete, unfragmented soul that has not reincarnated. Because the soul has many aspects that can act independently, these fragments of the whole often linger and retain the identity of a reincarnated soul or person. This often occurs when the soul needs to move on yet has obligations to others, especially unresolved relationships. The term "soul fragment" can mean the above or refer to other people or beings who share the same soul essence as yours (this is further explained on page 136).

Occasionally, a loved one who has serious karmic lessons to learn after physical death is unable to see a family member. For example, a fellow soul traveler I met during astral projection tried to see his father with whom he had a sad and interrupted relationship. The father abandoned his family while he was alive and, in simple but blunt terms, did not earn the right to see his son after death. This and similar situations seem like punishment but, in actuality, do not last forever. My friend was able to have one brief meeting with his father, but an ongoing relationship is not yet possible. Some issues were resolved so, until they see each other again, the meeting served to be a new beginning.

As you travel within the transitional plane, aside from seeing loved ones, with experience you may also learn how to help troubled souls cross over the threshold of death. As explained earlier, there are spirits who cannot let go of negative thought forms of living, which in turn creates a psychic wall that separates the spirit from loved ones and soul guides. The spirit cannot accept death and its process because it still clings to the earth and the life that was lived there. This is where you can become a spirit helper, even though you are still living.

I worked as a helper for a few years, and I was thrown into it quite unexpectedly by a sneaky but determined soul guide. During one of my journeys with my guide, we met a young woman who had taken her life by swallowing a poisonous substance. There were many spirits surrounding her, but she was so smothered with thought forms, she could not accept their assistance without first letting go. Apparently the pain of the death still lingered, and she was clutching her throat and screaming about the burning agony she was feeling in her body. My soul guide immediately seized the opportunity to speed my spiritual progress, and gave me a chance to earn my keep, so to speak, as a soul traveler. She told me to go over to her and explain that she was no longer in her body, that the pain was over. I protested like a wet hen and came up with a thousand reasons why I couldn't face such a pained soul. My guide answered me with a firm but loving push and, before I knew it, I was talking to this young woman as if I had prepared years to do it properly. I didn't even know where the words were coming from, but they were magical. In the long moments of speaking, in essence, I told her to remember her life as if she were viewing a movie. She was now detached, weightless, and independent of the events. The woman went from a hysterical state to a completely serene one in a matter of minutes. As she calmed, I saw thought forms flee from her like frightened birds. It was as if a great vacuum was sucking them into the ether. That day was to be one of many where I put my soul travel ability to good use and, in turn, learned valuable spiritual lessons that helped me immensely in my own life.

The issue of suicide has come up frequently during my travels. I can say without hesitation that each spirit I encountered who had taken their own life bitterly and desperately regretted it. It is not an issue of punishment or losing one's soul, the first being unlikely while the latter is impossible. However, it is an issue of running away from something only to crash right into it. For example, I met Greg. He was in his early thirties when he died by his own hand because he wanted to escape the ravages of AIDS. He was a beautiful soul who did not go to a lower realm of punishment but believed he had outwitted the inevitability of illness. It is the natural law of the universe: All that is avoided is eventually confronted; every thought and action has a corresponding result. So, the very thing that Greg killed himself to avoid turned out to be his karmic fate. Many spirits choose their own incarnations, but some, like Greg, get incarnations assigned to them. Rapidly, Greg's soul essence went into a baby who was to be born with the AIDS virus. Since Greg's new incarnation as an ill child was so brief, after death he was able to step into the identity known as Greg once more. It was then he told me his story. He could not emphasize enough the importance of facing situations you cannot avoid because suicide is only a false hope. If you were truly meant to experience a given situation, there is no escape, and even death cannot change your fate.

Judging from the spirits I spoke with, those who died by violent suicides always went to a hell world briefly before moving on. The word "briefly" does not describe that experience. All of them who did go to a lower realm said that it felt like a lifetime. And those who died with calm emotions or by gentler means all said that their evolution and spiritual progress were seriously retarded due to their actions. No matter how much pain we experience through living, we are meant to fulfill our purpose. It's like flunking a grade in school; the longer we avoid learning the lessons, the longer we'll be in the same place.

Whether you become a spirit helper or not, you will see many inspiring things within the transitional plane. You will see many spirits preparing for a new life on earth. Within this plane there is a realm where all you see is child spirits, some very much like the children next door while others hold great wisdom and spiritual knowledge. During a trying time in my physical life, I took an afternoon nap to make up for nights spent without sleep. During the nap, I projected to this realm within the transitional plane and spent an hour with the most beautiful, happy children I have ever seen. They took me as their willing playmate and we swam in aquamarine pools sparkling with gold light. I laughed until I forgot the seriousness of my own life. I returned to my physical body feeling completely well, happy, and transformed.

Also within the transitional realm are countless healing centers or temples where you can go when traditional medicine fails. These centers are filled with spirit physicians who use cosmic sound and color vibration to heal physical, emotional, and spiritual illness. It was here where I went to seek help for a lifelong stomach ailment. After four or so journeys to these temples, I was physically blessed with a healing that was nothing short of a spiritual miracle. However, sometimes we are supposed to experience certain things, including health problems, and it is not always possible that we can be gifted with a healing. I have other physical ailments I have tried to resolve, both in the physical world and the invisible worlds, to no avail. If you do decide to seek spiritual help there, do so with great faith. If you are healed, then it is a blessing to always cherish. If not, try to understand that your physical illness is still needed for certain lessons.

Overall, subplanes included, the transitional plane is not heaven, as so many people believe when they go there during near-death experiences. Heaven, or the afterlife, is all of the planes, subplanes, and realms that are of the light. Each has its own world within worlds, its function, its inhabitants, and its beauty. In a way, there are many heavens, like many mansions in our Father's house.

The transitional realm, unlike the finer planes following it, has its own cycles of day and night that mirror the earth plane. Beautiful sunrises, sunsets, summer twilights, and moonlit nights can all be witnessed within this plane. There is much to explore here, but as you travel to higher realms, you will find yourself continuously amazed at the intensity of beauty, color, and sound. There are realms so fine and brilliant that you would be crushed if you were unable to enter them. This is why the highest of the realms cannot always be found. But those planes that are accessible have infinite nooks and crannies of breathtaking beauty. Let's take a look at them.

Plane of Creative Force

The second of the higher worlds is the plane of creative force. The realms within this plane vibrate with exquisite sound, music, color, and light. This plane is undoubtedly my favorite because of the ecstasy felt when traveling through it. There are no words to describe the feeling of this world; it can only be experienced firsthand.

The entire plane, including subplanes and realms, is drenched in such a deep shade of afternoon gold that you breathe in light instead of air. Every spirit and every location is bathed in glimmering gold that resembles the waning bronze of the sun just before it dips below the horizon. Everywhere you go within this plane you find astonishing beauty that ignites your soul.

117

The plane of creative force is created and sustained by sound and color vibration alone. Just as food, water, and air keep us alive, these aesthetic components give life to this plane and its inhabitants. There are strange but beautiful sound languages that are "spoken" here, not for communication but rather for vibrational purposes. Cosmic sound, music, harmony, and vivid color rays heard, spoken, seen, and felt within this realm are essentially the creative force of the Ultimate Deity. This fire of divine creativity manifests worlds and all works of emotionally inspired art.

As you travel through this plane, you will seem to journey not with your thoughts but with your feelings. Every part of your soul body vibrates as a result of the creative forces materializing through intensity of beauty. You will see glittering rivers of dazzling colors with sparkling beds of clarion crystals. Many times I swam in rose pink waters until the fragrance and glimmering brilliant crystal beds put me into a pure trance of ecstasy.

Among the infinite number of breathtaking things you will see are amber-lit orchards dripping with succulent fruit with exquisite nectar tasting like peach, mango, tangerine, and pineapple combined. For many years, during periods of illness, my mother withstood terrible diet restrictions, but within these orchards she found solace and healing.

Among the inhabitants you may find here are inner plane artists, healers, teachers, and semi-divine beings of perfected loveliness. An order of angelic energies who blesses others with the divine fire of creativity and inspiration dwells within the plane of creative force. Our human description has led us to call them muses, and this is fine by them. They love to be called on to stir the flames of new ideas.

Most importantly, this plane and its subplanes are the dwelling places of many gods, goddesses, and demigods. There are other divinities who reside within the higher light realms, but those found on this plane strictly sustain acts of creation and ecstasy. I have encountered the unforgettable energy of Dionysus here (the Dionysian ray), so if you see a shimmering being with the form of perfected youth, flame-blue eyes, and a dark river of hair draped in deep purple light, you will know who it is. If and when you discover his presence, completely surrender and allow your soul body to absorb his powerful energy. You will enter a state of ecstasy for long moments that will leave you weak with deep emotion. Don't be afraid of the intensity of the experience, since it penetrates all of your senses—emotional, spiritual, as well as sexual. After you return to your body, do not be surprised if you have a hunger to create something beautiful or emotional.

Within these sound realms, you may come across a particularly large celestial city devoted to spiritual healing through sound, vibration, and color. The city's crystalline, cathedral-like structure shines in the deepest shade of rose. Its illuminated brilliance is intensified by the countless light beings who inhabit this etheric city.

If and when you find this extraordinary place, you may also see countless light ships descending and ascending. Many times these beings enter our physical realm and we believe them to be beings from other planets. Yes, there are other beings in and beyond our solar system, but some actually are of etheric reality. These light ships and light beings are so beautiful, they will take your breath away.

This city, called Teesha in the sound language of this plane, is open to your exploration. Within its walls you will probably also see many other spirits who practice, receive, and learn spiritual healing arts. I know a bit about this sprawling city because it is there where I most often see my father. Like others who have evolved to a certain level, he uses his special gifts as a tool for his own advancement as well as the advancement of those he comes in contact with.

If you find Teesha, be sure to journey through one of the immense meadows that encircles the city. Each flower within these fields radiates a different shade of spellbinding pink. The culmination of these flower energies creates a cosmos of perfumed lights ranging from the palest blush of dawn pink to the deepest kiss of fuchsia. Once you see these light gardens, no other earthly garden will look quite the same way again because you realize that, beyond the physical structure of all plants and flowers, the same light energy is always present.

Though it is impossible to know the entirety of this vast plane of creative force, any wonders you will harness will give you unforgettable soul memories.

Plane of Pure Thought

If you become accustomed to traveling up to the third plane, you will eventually be able to pass into the fourth plane. However, it may take practice as well as opening specific chakra centers. In order to travel within the finer spiritual realms, which begin with the fourth plane (plane of pure thought), a soul traveler must raise his or her vibrational level to that of the particular plane.

To gain access to the fourth plane, first travel to the third plane, the plane of creative force. Within the third plane, open the throat and brow chakras by placing both hands on each center and move them in a clockwise direction. (Review: Clockwise direction for opening, counterclockwise for closing.) As you move your hands in a clockwise direction over the chakra, visualize light beaming from your palms into the center. Do this with both the throat and brow chakras until you feel expansion or warmth in those areas. Once you feel that your psychic centers are open or stimulated, direct yourself by thought into the fourth plane. You may simply repeat to yourself, "The fourth plane or the plane of pure thought."

Sometimes a soul traveler can try and try and still not be able to enter the higher realms. If this happens to you, simply stop trying and continue to travel to those planes that you can travel to with ease. By doing this, you will gain more experience and, by doing so, your vibrational level will rise enough so it matches finer worlds. Be sure to also remain on a serious but joyous spiritual path by doing spiritual work daily. That can also give you more chances to be successful.

The plane of pure thought houses all finite and infinite knowledge. This plane is a mecca for spiritual seekers due to its innumerable etheric libraries, universities, and learning spaces solely devoted to spiritual and intellectual sciences, elevated arts, and philosophies inspired by the higher mind or spiritual devotion.

The Akashic Records, the most vast and significant of spiritual libraries, can be found within the fourth plane. This celestial "hall of records" holds soul information of every person, entity, and spirit of all planes of existence including events, past lives, future lives, and happenings. Because of its value and its elevated vibrational level, only a chosen few can earn the privilege to explore its etheric contents. If you are one of the few, you will be able to do so but probably only with the aid of one of the masters found within its vastness.

No matter which learning center or library you explore on the fourth plane and its subplanes, you will not read in the usual way. Instead, you may simply put your hand on a volume of information and automatically know its contents. This strange but wonderful type of psychic osmosis is also experienced in the spiritual universities. Telepathy and visual manifestations are a teacher's primary aids. You may see huge screens on which thoughts, like riveting films, are created.

The landscape of this plane is very intense in color, and light emanates from every spirit and structure. All libraries and universities here are beyond human comprehension or design. All of them I have seen appear as polished crystal, gleaming gemstone, or pure diamond-bright light. The environment, though, is constantly changing and transforming due to the infinite number of thought energies interacting simultaneously. Each time I visit the fourth plane, I witness objects, structures, even mountains appear or disappear in front of me within a breath of a second.

The inhabitants of the fourth plane and its subplanes are numerous but you may encounter great teachers, philosophers, inventors, scientists, composers, artists, and advanced guides. Some have been known on the physical plane while others have never experienced a human form and life. All I have encountered were kind, but a few were also very advanced and unapproachable, not out of supremacy but simple vibrational differences.

Plane of Being

Only advanced soul travelers are able to reach the fifth plane and then only for brief periods of time. The fifth plane, the plane of being, can only be reached by transforming your spirit body into a light form. This can only be done by intense will, chakra stimulation, or melding with the energy of an advanced soul. Since going into a light body requires a great deal of experience and a high vibrational level, it can only be accomplished when the time is spiritually right for you. Then you will simply imagine yourself as light, and you will be light. Until then, you may try the melding method to transform into light energy (this technique is discussed in detail in Chapter 8). I do not discuss it here because it involves a thorough explanation of spirit lovers and cosmic mates and the nature of the cosmic relationship.

If you have reached the fourth plane, the plane of pure thought, then you may wish to attempt going into a light form by opening and closing certain chakras. This may be more difficult than the melding method, but it may work well for you. While you are within the fourth plane, close all chakras except the brow and crown chakras. To close centers, place both hands over each chakra and move them in a counterclockwise direction while imagining light beaming from your palms into the center. Once you feel a sensation of tightness, the chakra is closed or no longer stimulated. Do this all the way to the brow. Then open or stimulate the brow chakra by placing both hands over the center and moving them in a clockwise direction while visualizing light beaming from your palms into the chakra. When you feel expansion in the area or see light energy shining from within the chakra, the center is open. Do the same with the crown chakra. Once both chakras are open, stimulated, and emanating radiant light, focus solely on the light at the top of your head. Imagine yourself in the light. Once you do this, you may automatically transfer your consciousness into the light and become light. If it doesn't happen the first time, you may wish to practice this often. When you do accomplish becoming a light form, you will then be pure consciousness, without form, identity, or conception of time. You will be free, fluid, and untouchable as fire. There are no words to describe being a spirit of divine light. Returning to your usual spirit form is as simple as willing it. There is no danger of becoming lost or stuck in a light body. IMPORTANT: Always be sure to open all chakras that you closed before returning to your physical body via the method of clockwise hand/light rotation.

The fifth plane of being is the home of masters, advanced souls, fine light beings, and light energies. Since it is of such fine etheric matter, remembering your journey may be very difficult. Once you again enter the previous realms and the physical world of time, your consciousness is no longer able to retain or understand the sights, sounds, energies, and purpose of the fifth plane. The activity of this light plane is incomprehensible to any mind still ruled by time or fulfilling karmic obligations in a physical body, so don't be dismayed if you return with only feelings or brief images of the plane of being.

Plane of Energy

It is highly unlikely that any of us can travel to this heaven world, save for a chosen few who have the inborn evolvement and soul advancement necessary for access. It is unnecessary to enter this plane to receive its knowledge or benefits because its inhabitants, angelic intelligences and light gods (including Avatars, advanced beings), most often appear on a lower plane in order to communicate with a particular soul. When they do appear on another plane for communication, these divine energies most often appear androgynous, but there are exceptions (all gender identification dissolves from the fifth plane onward, though you may see androgynous beings on any plane).

The sixth plane is the realm of the celestial hierarchy, including all orders of advanced angels, masters, and manifestations of the Ultimate Deity (god and goddess energies). These energies are all accessible on other planes below the sixth, so do not feel that because this plane is most often unreachable it is not relevant to us. This plane, like all of the others, interacts with all of existence. Everything is part of the whole; there are no divisions.

Plane of the Unknown

The final plane is the birthing place of all manifested reality, physical or etheric. It is ruled by the Ultimate Deity, who is beautifully unknowable and who sustains all of creation. We cannot hope to enter into the seventh world until we are transformed by death. Only then will we know its mysteries. But whenever we travel to any plane or acknowledge the beauty of our physical world, we get a glimpse of the power and purpose of this Ultimate Source.

Now that you have an idea of what is possible through soul travel, you may wish to take your ability a step further by entering the lover's world. Part Two discusses in depth the reality of spirit lovers, cosmic mates, soul mates, and melding and lovemaking in the spirit world.

The Soul Traveler as Lover

Chapter Six

The Eternal Heart

Astral Lovers, Cosmic Mates,
and Love's Divinity

In the immortal myth "Psyche and Eros," a beautiful young woman is cursed by Aphrodite, the Greek goddess of love. The curse is that she is fated to marry a monster. Out of envy for the comely mortal woman, Aphrodite orders her son Eros to fulfill her wishes. All goes well until Eros wounds himself with one of his own golden arrows and falls in love with the beautiful and gentle Psyche.

Within each soul, an angel sleeps,
> Nestled in oblivion
> Until a Lover wakes its dreaming . . .
> What is love
> But the awakening of the divinity
> In ourselves?

Just as Psyche is to arrive at the monster's home, Eros tells the west wind to intervene and carry her to his own homeland instead. There, Psyche is waited on like royalty from invisible servants. She is fed food fit only for the gods and dressed in luxurious garments that befit her radiant loveliness. Every wish is granted, but Psyche never sees who is waiting on her.

Later, she is introduced to her new husband, who is also invisible to her. He tells her that all he has within his prosperous kingdom is hers, under one condition: that she should never ask to see his face. And so they begin a beautiful marriage despite the fact that Psyche can only be with her husband in complete darkness.

After seeing her family members, she is convinced by them that her husband is actually the monster she was fated to wed. Psyche obeys the voice of doubt and enters her husband's sleeping chamber. Within her shaking hands, Psyche holds a knife and a lamp to guide her. Intent on slaying the repulsive beast, Psyche leans over her husband with the raised dagger but in the lamplight the truth is revealed. Not only is her husband not a monster, but the beautiful white-winged god of love. Psyche is so overcome with joy that her hands falter and a drop of burning oil from her lamp falls onto Eros' bare shoulder. Eros awakens to find his wife's mistrust and betrayal and flies into the night with unfurled brilliant wings.

After a long, treacherous path of despair, trickery, and hopelessness, Psyche falls into a death sleep. Eros, having watched his bride and invisibly come to her aid along the way, can no longer withstand not being with her. With betrayal forgotten, Eros awakens Psyche and takes her to Olympus, the snow-capped home of the gods. There he feeds her ambrosia and nectar, the fare of immortality. The lovers reunite, and Psyche gives birth to their daughter, Pleasure.

The Greek word for soul is "psyche," and the word for love is "eros." This timeless myth represents the mystical marriage of the Divine Self and the eternal heart in each of us. We become greater only through love. Only through love can we glimpse the immortal part of ourselves. Also apparent in this myth is the pain along the path we must often endure before we meet our true beloved and earn the right to spiritual power.

To me, the myth of Psyche and Eros has always been representative of the secret double life many mystics lead. These lives are often conducted in the spirit body and are never spoken of. Like the tribal shaman, a mystic may find partners within the spirit realm rather than exclusively relating to physical companions. Due to their vocation, calling, and daily existence that is totally immersed in the unseen worlds, it is not surprising that their love relationships are also of a mysterious and mystical nature.

Many spiritually dedicated people desire to lead solitary lives to pursue the rapture of the spirit but find it difficult to sacrifice companionship and sexual expression with a beloved. A very good friend of mine who is a brilliant metaphysician and medium once laughed when I told him, a bit cautiously, that I had a cosmic partner. "Of course! Many, many mystics lead double lives—it's commonplace." Needless to say, it gave me great reassurance and peace to find that there were others who experienced this phenomenon.

There are probably many of you who are reading this who have experienced a cosmic relationship or who would like to. Yes, you can continue to have physical relationships while you have spiritual relationships or you may choose to fully embrace the mystic's life. The latter is not necessary to realize your full potential but is simply a lifestyle that is indeed possible. It is possible to be physically celibate while experiencing a full and beautiful sensual life within the invisible worlds via soul travel. Anyone who wishes to spend weeks, months, or years on a complete spiritual quest that involves being partnerless can actually enhance his or her progress by forming a cosmic relationship.

No matter what relationship you are in, physical or mystical, if it is a channel for pure love and communication, then you already know the spiritual power possible through the soul mate experience. When two lovers share the same vibrational frequency and become instruments of divine energy through their communication, shared passions, and lovemaking, then love can be the passage to enlightenment. There is no greater spiritual purity on any plane than the love shared between two lovers when they are deeply and unconditionally in love.

Throughout time, the thread that runs through most religions is the concept of love. All love is equal and divine when it is pure. Contrary to the human understanding of love as emotion, in essence, love is energy. Energy is God, God is love; we are energy, we are love. When we surrender ego and fear, we can become like reeds in the wind and allow love to pass through us. It is then we can create with this energy and even manifest miracles.

This wonderful and simple knowledge, though, can be difficult to believe when we walk down the street or flick on the television. We are constantly reminded that we are living in a time where love has been reduced to soap opera romance, pornography, and one- night stands with strangers. We are also constantly equating love with fear because of the threat of AIDS and STDs. Like the mythological gods of antiquity, love has become a lovely and poetic ideal that is rarely believed in, aspired to and, most of all, rarely understood.

Because love has become a battlefield, we must become spiritual warriors and individually invoke the power of love in our lives. Each person, each beloved is a ripple on the surface of the pond that begets another. Perhaps this is the nucleus of all religious or mystical quests: to reach a state of love, and then all else is possible. But to accomplish this, all doubt and fear must first be conquered or the pristine consciousness of love will be diluted.

Despite the prosperity and joy of her union with Eros, Psyche still doubted the identity of her husband. Instead of doing what Psyche did in the myth, we must have faith in the fact that love is our birthright and our destiny if we only allow it to find us. Every day we hear ourselves say, "I'll never find a soul mate—it's just not in the cards for me." Or, when we do find that soulful, beautiful partner, we say, "It's not going to last—it's too good." When we enter love's space with lamp and dagger, it is always scared away. It is like trying to call a wild bird to us. Only trust, gentleness, and patience guide the bird into the open palm.

Because of our modern feverish search for The One, we force love to take root and then wonder why it doesn't grow. All lovers who have found that elusive destined partner have one thing in common: it happened when they least expected it. This is not only the case with physical partnerships but with cosmic ones as well. When I was a teenager learning soul travel, I didn't set out to find a spirit lover. I didn't even know it was possible, much less probable, that I would experience it.

I did not pursue out-of-body relationships because I was bitter about physical relationships or because I was simply curious. It was part of my unfolding spiritual growth, as it still is. Needless to say, there were times when I doubted my own sanity, felt isolated because I could not tell anyone and, most of all, believed that I was the only one who had experienced love in other worlds.

Since those awkward and lonely years, I have met others who have also lived this aspect of the mystical life. Like me, they are sound in mind and body, have their work, circles of friends, and fit into normal society. Some are married or have serious partners in their physical life. Some have children and active family lives. No matter what our differences are, the nature of the cosmic relationship is the same. From my own experience and the experience of those I have known and spoken with, there are two basic types of spiritual partners, cosmic mates and astral lovers. Let's begin with the latter.

Astral Lovers

An astral lover is any person or spirit you have a love relationship with via soul travel. Astral lovers can be of either sex and from any plane of existence. They may be living and fulfilling an earthly destiny or they may be living in a different dimension, physical or etheric. Those who are living may be fully conscious of the relationship while others may not retain the memory of their spirit's activities.

Relationships with living astral lovers mirror physical partnerships concerning commitment, emotional baggage, and every positive and negative aspect common to everyday unions. The same poignancy, satisfaction, and multi-faceted nuances are experienced, as well as the pain, betrayal, and misunderstandings. Just because the relationship does not involve petty issues such as who's paying for dinner or who forgot to buy milk after work does not mean that everything is perfect. Just because the universe offers more simplicity and opportunity than the local club on Friday night, relationships with astral lovers are not guaranteed to be free of frustrations or necessarily made from the stuff "forever" is made from.

Because the soul body is free to don any chosen appearance and, because it is easier to get away with not being ourselves in the invisible worlds, it is also easier to become involved with someone who is not right for us. Just as we have to watch for opportunists, con artists, and too-good-to-be-true dates in the physical world, we have to watch for the same in the astral. It is important to enter any relationship—cosmic or earthly—for the right reasons.

If you have not experienced a partnership with an astral lover, you may have a lot of questions, such as, "Where do you meet? Where do you go? How often are you together? How do you know where to find each other? How can someone be having an astral relationship and not know it?" I hope my story answers some of these questions.

When I was sixteen, I attended my tenth-grade classes, went to the lake with my best girlfriend, and listened to my favorite music. Save for my mother and father, no one knew that I also left my body during study hall, spoke to my soul guide after I got off the bus in the afternoon, and experienced love interests in both worlds.

As I reached my seventeenth year, I fell in love for the first time, but it was a silent passage. I could not tell friends about my significant other. I couldn't introduce him to my parents. I couldn't bring home little sentimental souvenirs from our times together. I couldn't call him on the phone. But for four years, I left my body daily to be with him.

His name was Dorian, and he was much older than myself. Due to the fact that, as we live our physical lives, there are other parts of the soul that exist and function on other planes for the purpose of experience beyond our comprehension and remembrance, Dorian was not physically aware of his inner life. Yes, he was living a normal life in the physical world and had no idea of the activities of his spirit, but our relationship was like any other. We had creative interests and spiritual studies in common as well as similar emotional needs. We traveled to light realms, kissed on the streets of San Francisco, and made love during New England twilights while snow began to fall. It was four years that molded me as a person. Like any first love, I thought it would last forever and that I would die without him; but we parted ways, and I learned much through his gentleness and brilliance.

As my spiritual life brought me into deeper waters, I made the choice to have love relationships via soul travel. The choice was made effortlessly, perhaps for me. It fit my life, my mind, my heart, my philosophy. It brought me great challenges and growth and, above all, the greatest joy I had ever known. It has been many years since I first saw Dorian's restless green eyes, and only now can I say that I have finally found the spiritual partner whom I can truly call a soul twin. I have also found what I call a cosmic mate, which differs from an astral lover but is also the most exciting subject of spiritual relationships, which I will discuss shortly.

Meeting an astral lover on any plane usually happens out of the blue. Like minds and like souls attract one another like magnets once out of the physical body. Since this law of affinity is unavoidable, two souls usually just meet up one day and the rest is unstoppable. You can plan to meet somewhere on the following journey, but most of the time it is unnecessary. A like soul always knows where another is, especially if the bond and the love are deep.

How often you see an astral lover depends solely on the harmony of physical schedules and choice. Usually meetings begin weekly or even monthly and can evolve to a daily occurrence. Many partnerships are born during nocturnal soul journeys and then graduate to conscious meetings. Each relationship is different, though, due to the diversity of experiences and opportunities in the soul body.

Someone asked me if you can meet someone astrally and then arrange to meet them physically. I have never personally experienced this, but it is indeed possible if both parties are fully aware of what is going on. Only then can both worlds meet without confusion, disappointment, or misleadings.

Homosexuality is common within the spirit realms, as it is on the earth plane, but since all gender identification drops from the fifth plane onward, gay relationships are experienced and witnessed on all planes below the fifth. Same-sex partnerships are not different from any other, but issues of polarity do earn special attention.

Due to the fact that relationships with astral lovers are as intense or even more intense than physical relationships, sometimes it is difficult to balance your physical life with your astral life, especially if you are physically committed to someone else. Since the soul is free and is not bound to earthly concepts, having a soul lover and a physical partner is not unethical, but it can be very complex. This is why it is imperative to keep one foot firmly in the physical. This includes never comparing your astral lover with your husband, wife, girlfriend, or boyfriend. Whether your astral companion is a better listener or a better lover does not matter. Your physical commitment is what matters because that relationship takes most of your time, energy, and consciousness. If you find that you cannot balance both, eliminate the astral partner or find a middle ground.

Telling a skeptical or possessive spouse about your astral relationships can and may cause trouble, so be cautious as to how and when you share your experiences. If and when you do, remember to always be considerate and respectful toward your physical partner. Don't give him or her an impossible perfect rival they feel that they have to live up to. My best advice is to keep your astral relationship part of your spiritual life, which means that it should be treated as sacred, whatever you choose to do.

Most importantly, don't expect your physical partnership to equal your astral union. Bills, rent, car trouble, in-laws, children, and outside influences are not part of the spiritual relationship so, because of these things alone, it will be a smoother journey of the heart. Bear this in mind when you want to compare the two.

Occasionally, you may meet someone who won't leave you alone. Most of the time, these astral partners back off, but some can get psychically dangerous. If this happens, use the severance technique in Chapter 1.

Cosmic Mates

A cosmic mate is usually of the opposite sex and is your ultimate spiritual counterpart. Unlike some astral lovers, cosmic mates are always not living but have attained great advancement within the invisible worlds of spirit.

Each person has a cosmic mate. You and your cosmic mate share the same spiritual DNA, so to speak. You are both harmonious soul equals and, during the course of your evolvement, share the same map of karmic experience. This parallel of soul lessons may bring you together during lifetimes, but one or both of you must advance considerably within the inner worlds before you can truly be together. This is why cosmic mates are more difficult to pursue, but it can be accomplished.

Soul Mates and Soul Fragments

When we meet someone who seems to be an identical extension of ourselves, we often are coupled with a soul mate or a soul fragment. A soul mate is someone we have shared many lifetimes with, but there can be more than one during a current lifetime. All of us encounter many soul mates, not just one. And, contrary to belief, a soul mate can also change roles and, instead of being our lover, they can be a beloved family member.

On the other side of the coin, a soul fragment is someone who shares the same soul essence as yours. Sometimes during the course of evolution, a soul essence splits, sometimes more than once for added karmic or earthly experience. These splits or fragments of ourselves become independent souls. Often, those who are fortunate are reunited with these fragments and the relationship is blessed with deep like-mindedness, communication, and familiarity.

Those times we are with a soul mate or soul fragment, we may think that we are with a cosmic mate but, more often than not, that is not the case. Occasionally your cosmic mate is still experiencing an earthly body and life at the same time you are, but most of the time they have already moved on within other realms. Once your reincarnation cycle is completed on this plane, you and your cosmic mate will ultimately join spiritual forces and become like one soul. But the really good news about this is that through soul travel, you can contact your cosmic mate now. Though, due to many reasons, you and that spirit may not be able to truly be together now, you can still have incredible experiences and meetings with him or her.

Relationships with cosmic mates—unlike other astral relationships, no matter how perfect—are completely free of negative aspects such as jealousy, obligation, possessiveness, and selfishness. There is an unspoken knowledge of each other's needs, a mystical understanding of souls that transcends rational thought. Many times words are literally superfluous. Passion is unequaled, save for the profound physical or astral relationship with a soul mate or fragment. Above all, the energy that is received from knowing and loving a cosmic mate is energy that can create miracles, healing, and transformation in your life. Once this spiritual power is tapped, your growth on all levels can reach undreamed-of heights.

Sanschi, my cosmic mate, entered my life during my early twenties. It was during a dark night of the soul when he stepped into my world as gently as a leaf onto water and changed my life forever with his influence. Glimpsing his smile, I knew that he was my soul's ultimate destination; all journeys, dreams, spiritual purpose, and experience were ships that finally found the harbor of his eyes.

Only moments after meeting him for the first time on a fragrant October night, I knew I had found my shadow self as we flew into the darkness. Breast to breast, we soared to the stars; all past heartaches, triumphs, and disappointments fell like ashes as I glanced at the spinning earth below us.

Night after night, pressed to Sanschi's warm heart, I traveled to realms more beautiful and brilliant than I had ever imagined. We fused our soul energies together in explosions of prismatic light and ecstasy. We swam in light-shimmering pools, made love beneath thundering waterfalls, and drank bliss from each other's presence.

Each morning I filled pages of a journal with the night's happenings. With his instruction, I learned how to leave the body through the heart center, work with discarnates, project my consciousness without preparation, and see the world through fearless eyes.

During the months that followed, my creativity soared like never before as I would feel his tremendous energy actually filter through my body. I had more energy and stamina than I had ever known. This awakening included a powerful sexual awakening that allowed me to embrace the male energy in my life without fear or emotional issues. The beauty of his spirit, the chiseled alabaster features, the profusion of soft, dark hair, the dawn blue of his penetrating eyes all left me breathless. The depth of ecstasy of this union reminded me of the pure and true Dionysian experience of the Greeks.

Due to the fact that I was not committed to a physical partner, I found it easy to sustain my relationship with Sanschi, despite our two different worlds. Though he is part of my every day and my ultimate spiritual destiny will be in him, I am now also involved with another astral lover who nourishes my creativity and needs that only someone from this plane can fully identify with. I now believe that this lover and partner, whom I believe to be a soul fragment, could not have entered my life if not for the powerful lessons of love I learned with Sanschi. The productive and exciting years spent with Sanschi have molded me into the type of person who is now ready to accept love as well as love myself. Perhaps this is the most valuable lesson I have learned from my cosmic mate.

Chelsea, a fellow soul traveler, had experiences with a cosmic mate very similar to mine. At the time of her encounter, she was a wife and mother struggling to balance her needs with the needs of her husband and children while completing a challenging university program. Her husband was living in another state due to career obligations, and the responsibility of holding her family together left Chelsea exhausted both physically and mentally. During this trying period of her life, on a typically ordinary night, Chelsea's life changed forever. In her own words, this is her story.

It was a challenging day. A test was due, both children had colds, and the car needed repair. After an hour of tossing and turning, I drifted into a state of semiconsciousness. I found myself in my spirit body and completely aware of my surroundings.

While walking the streets of a vaguely familiar etheric city, I glanced up from my meandering and looked into limpid blue eyes. Instantaneous recognition! At that moment, I knew this being was the missing part of my life. There was no need for trivial courtesies or courtship. We flowed into one another's arms, two ancient friends together again. I was home at last. None of my daily concerns existed. No tests, no kids, no husband.

Together, we strode a path away from the city through a thicket of wildflowers and clover. We laughed, cried, and whispered of our longing for this moment. We lived and loved in the eternal moment of our togetherness. I rediscovered the immensity of universal love.

The azure sky was the backdrop for this beautiful, golden man who leaned over me, gazing at me earnestly. His hair was flaxen, skin tawny. I offered no resistance, but fused completely into his being. His golden aura enveloped us both, making us truly one. Our heartbeats were synchronized. I heard them beating in unison. Lips, arms, legs all melded together in a feeling beyond orgasmic. It was ecstasy in its purest form, a moment of rapture beyond comprehension. I was completely dissolved into his pure and aeriferous light.

The next moment, I bolted upright in bed with the name Adrianni on my lips. Was it a dream? No! I knew this being with every rhythm of my physical self. I lay in bed until dawn, basking in the incandescence of his ardor. I felt no guilt or shame. It had been the highest form of spiritual expression.

In the ensuing weeks following that night, we met sporadically. Never quite knowing which nights would be ours, I often drifted off to sleep with my dream-lover's name on my lips. Whenever he arrived, I always felt Adrianni's energy first. It was the most familiar of all feelings, like recognizing my own image while passing a mirror.

When we greeted one another, waves of devotion, awe, longing, and desire passed between us. Strangely, we never spoke of our pasts. I emphasize "spoke" because I cannot recall using much verbal language with Adrianni. All was understood between us on a level beyond speech. Yet I can still recall his voice, musical, mellow, baritone.

Our trysts felt like healings. We explored wonderful ethereal places unlike anything I've seen on earth—palaces of learning with tremendous libraries, lecture rooms, stairwells leading to other levels. Each plane was rich in art, sculpture, and radiant light. Looking down from the terraces, we saw cerulean pools bedecked with rainbow flowers generating color as energy, brilliant against verdant shrubbery and cobalt skies.

Unfailingly, we ended each excursion alone in each other's arms. It was beyond passion. It was the spark of creation, the union of soul and soul, a connection to the source of life. Our energies melded in an eruption of pleasure and awareness.

After our meldings, I always awoke alone, trembling in the darkness, longing once again for my empyrean friend. Sometimes I questioned my sanity. Here I was, an educated married woman, a mother, yearning for a love I could not touch, see, or smell during the day. My ambivalence was short-lived, however, for always during my moments of highest doubt, Adrianni would return, reassuring me that I wasn't crazy. To add to his support, I realized something profound had happened to me. I had been transformed from frightened to intrepid and congenial. I was happier. Each day was a challenge, each night a reward. My children responded to their more capable mother and my husband was intrigued by his revitalized wife. I harbored no dissatisfaction with my husband as our love seemed strengthened by my supernal affair.

One night during a fervent embrace near pounding surf, the scent of the sea pervasive, the stars enclosing us, I understood that my Adrianni would no longer come to me in this way. My heart grieved for the loss but my mind rejoiced for the gain, for I knew that Adrianni has ever been and will ever be the missing hemisphere of my earthly existence. Yet, though I long for the physical embodiment of my great encounter, he is never completely distant and has returned during times of great distress.

My deterrent for mourning this love is the certainty that one day we will once again merge for eternity.

Chelsea's mesmerizing story is testimony of the power of love to transform, heal, complete, and enhance our lives, even if it is not given to us for an entire lifetime. Such a cosmic mate experience can be utterly consuming and, perhaps, Adrianni did not want Chelsea to ever feel divided between his ethereal love and her life experiences with her physical husband and family.

To be blessed with a cosmic relationship with any person or being and experience passion, ecstasy, and unity of this magnitude, we must first light the lamp of love within ourselves. Psyche, or the soul, must first be willing to become an empty vessel that will be filled with the beloved. True beauty and deep sexual expression cannot be fully known until we recognize that we are worthy of true, bountiful love. Only then can we hope to glimpse destiny with a longed-for partner on any plane.

Most of the time, astral love relationships happen without preparation or pursuit, but if you would like to give Fate a good nudge, then the next chapter will be beneficial to you.

$\mathcal{H}eart\text{-}\mathcal{Q}uest$

Finding a

Spirit Lover

With or without our acknowledgment, Nature goes about her business with supreme promptness. Everything is in perpetual order, even when we believe she is in chaos. Each and every one of her creatures has an inborn intelligence that is in silent partnership with the seasons. How do geese know the exact moment to fly south, how to get there, and when to return? How does the crocus know that it is safe to peek through cold earth, even though winter winds still make it feel that snow is on the way?

Soul Sister, Soul Brother,
I see you in the stars
And hear your voice in the sea.
You are unknown, but I think of you
When I walk down a windy highway,
Knowing somewhere, you walk a road
Leading into mine . . . .

The voice of the Infinite whispers within bird and flower the same way it whispers within us, though we are less inclined to listen. When we do listen to the inner voice and allow our lives to flow like rivers to the sea, unobstructed by doubt and fear, we get a glimpse of our own greatness. Just like the ebb and flow of nature, we too are in the right place at this very moment in time, no matter how terrible or wonderful it may be. When we realize this and surrender to the bends in the road, we gain ultimate control over our lives. The same conscious surrender is necessary in finding a partner, spiritual or otherwise.

If you are interested in finding a spirit lover, at this second, let the desire go. Send it out to the universe like a balloon with your name on it, and then forget about it. Don't hold onto it because harboring any desire hinders the natural flow of energy necessary for the result to return to you.

Find a quiet place and allow yourself a half hour to daydream just as you did when you were very young. Even if it feels awkward at first, work through it. See, hear, and feel your ideal spiritual partner. Do not envision someone you already know because this borders on psychic manipulation.

Imagine yourself at any location, such as the Louvre in Paris or on the banks of a sparkling etheric river on the third plane. Wherever you choose to imagine yourself to be, make sure the location reflects your interests and needs. Now picture yourself with a spirit partner. What does he or she look like? What are his or her interests? Imagine all of the details you possibly can. This is your daydream. This is your time to put a request into the suggestion box of the universe. Envision yourself with this partner doing activities you like to do. See yourself deeply loved for the real you. See yourself completely, happily, and healthily in love. I emphasize the word "in" because when we are truly in love, we are *inside* of love. See yourself meeting, knowing, and loving someone who is ideal for you.

Consistently daydream this whenever you can and leave or try to leave your body on a regular basis. If you are striving to meet someone in the dream state during sleep, use this visualization before bedtime. Don't give the universal energy mixed messages by having extreme confidence one day and utter self-doubt the next. Be optimistic and, above all, surrender to the will of the tides. The sea always returns what is offered on its waves, and the universe is no exception.

If someone had asked me five years ago or even two years ago to envision the perfect spirit partner for me, I would have visualized a tall, dark poet with hair like Shelley and a quiet, predictable nature. It would have helped if he meditated and memorized Walt Whitman. However, the universe knew my desires and needs more than I did. Today, I am with someone who is my creative and spiritual counterpart and is every dream I could have dreamt—but he isn't tall or dark. His hair is very short and doesn't look like Shelley's. His nature is as unpredictable as the winds, and the only meditation he does is his creative work. He can, though, quote Whitman and a lot of other poets and is brilliant beyond my expectations. So if a person shows up in your path or in your dreams unlike the image you put out, don't automatically assume he or she is not a destined partner. Like souls, like minds, and like needs always find each other.

I know people who do rituals to attract a mate on any level but, from my own personal experience, the safest and surest way to find a like-minded spirit partner is simple visualization over a period of time. Daydreaming is the most enjoyable and powerful form of visualization. With patience, you will find the right person at the right place and at the right time.

Attracting a Spirit Lover

Aside from daydreaming, the following activities can attract a spirit lover into your life:

Working with a Soul Guide

If you are in contact with one of your soul guides, ask him or her to guide you to the right person. Ask your guide where you should look for this person or spirit and when to pursue a relationship.

If you are not in conscious contact with a soul guide, ask the same questions to your guiding spirits in prayer. They may answer you in dreams, images, visions, or simple intervention. In either case, the following prayer or something similar is appropriate: "Dear guiding spirits and all spirits of light, help me to find a spirit partner who will help me to grow spiritually and emotionally. Please send me a brother or sister of soul and bless us with communication, love, passion, and friendship. Thank you." If you are Wiccan, you may wish to say this prayer to Aphrodite or Ishtar. If you are a follower of Eastern religion, you may wish to ask the Hindu god Ganesha to remove all of your obstacles to finding an ideal spirit lover.

Letter Writing

Another powerful but simple way to send your intention out into the universe is to write a heartfelt letter to your spirit partner. Make believe that the person who is destined to be your companion will read the letter. Tell him or her about yourself, what you look like, where you live, what your interests are, what your goals are, what your heartaches have been, what you need in a love relationship, why you want a spirit lover, where he or she can find you (choose an astral location), and how much you are looking forward to meeting him or her. Pour your soul into each word and then fold the letter into an envelope. You may wish to place the letter under the pillow you use for soul travel or sleep. Wherever you do put it, be sure to seal it and keep it from being discovered by anyone else. If you have an altar where you pray, meditate, or do rituals, place the letter there.

Don't re-open the letter until you find a spirit lover. Allow the universe to do its work without your anticipation.

Full Moon Ritual

The energies of attraction are strongest at the time of the waxing and full moon. To use these energies to bring love into your life, find an area indoors or out where you can sit in the brilliance of the moon. As you feel the moonlight bathing you with its beautiful silver beams, imagine what the moon has seen. Imagine the countless lovers of the ages who gazed on it and those it watched from the watchtower of the heavens.

As you feel aglow with the moon's light, imagine yourself with a spirit partner. Feel him or her by your side. See the moonlight painting the face of your lover. Know that by the time the moon is full again, you will have met a spirit whom you can talk to, travel with, learn with, and love with. Expect to meet him or her during a soul journey, even if it is during sleep. You will remember.

As you look at the sky, imagine your potential spirit lover somewhere also looking at the moon. Know that he or she needs and wants your love as much as you need and want his or hers. Speak to him or her, perhaps even using the following words:

> With each star's burning
> Night dreams on the billows.
> At this hour of love's yearning,
> My soul walks with your soul.

Imagine the night winds carrying your words and thoughts to your destined partner. Know without a doubt that somehow your spirit already made contact with your spirit lover, and it will only be a matter of time until you meet.

No matter which activity you choose to bring a spirit partner into your life, be sure to give it time and complete faith. Only visualize or do rituals when you feel positive and well, for negative vibrations from illness, depression, or frustration can attract the wrong partner to you.

Once you do meet someone, bear in mind what I have stressed throughout this book: Be cautious, especially when a powerful sexual attraction outweighs other emotions, and do not believe that every spirit you meet is a good or suitable partner or lover. Keep your thoughts spiritual, not sexual.

Once you do your part, wait for the universe to do its part. Don't be impatient, negative, or assuming. Remember, the person of your dreams will come in the physical and emotional package he or she is meant to come in; and after the fact, you will feel that he or she was custom-made for you. Above all, believe in the eternal power of love; of two halves finding one another to make a whole; of the fact that love is stronger than circumstance, worldly ties, and distance. Believe that love with a spirit partner is the most sacred and meaningful of loves. In this type of relationship, you are giving someone the most important thing and only thing you will ever own: your soul.

Chapter Eight

Dances of Ecstasy

Lovemaking and Melding

in the Soul Body

*I*n ancient times, the sensual and the sacred were looked upon as two halves of the same spiritual whole. Religion was deeply rooted in the celebration of the turning seasons, especially apparent in the fertility cults of Dionysus, Aphrodite, Astarte, Baal, and Bast. Seasonally observed, these ecstatic celebrations focused on the growth rhythms of the land and the deities thought responsible for the bounty.

Beloved, press my fruit to your hunger
So I may bleed my ecstasy and offer my divinity
For this hour, if only this hour,
I am immortal.

Celebrants left populated cities to revel in the wild. Dancing, drinking, and ecstatic music catalyzed sexual activity. Though madness replaced reason more often than not, for a chosen few the lack of inhibition cultivated by intoxicants and sound begot powerful mystical experiences. Any child conceived during these nights of ecstasy was believed to be a child of the Goddess.

Prostitution, now considered to be a degrading drain on society, was once a holy and respectable contribution to ancient matriarchal civilizations. Unlike the modern underworld of lust, greed, drug traffic, and abuse, ancient temple prostitution was a life of spiritual service to Deity. Servants of the Goddess, or temple prostitutes, entered a house of worship while they were young girls to learn the revered arts of ritual, dance, and adornment. Lifetime service and devotion to the Deity began with a ritual sacrifice of virginity. Any sexual act performed after this holy sacrifice was consecrated and dedicated to the Goddess. Men returned from war found pleasure as well as emotional healing in these priestesses. To have intercourse with a temple prostitute was to directly commune with the all-creating, all-knowing Mother of the Universe.

The office of temple priest was also thought of as holy. Boys entered the temple of a chosen Deity and led lives of devotion and service. The homosexual temple priest, or Kadosh of Babylonian cultures, also had a definitive place in society.

Medieval Hindu temples of India still awe and even shock those who visit these breathtaking testimonies of art, religion, and sacred sexuality. These elaborate temples are the remains of a forgotten time when pleasure of the body opened the gates to enlightenment and bliss. This concept of spiritual salvation was and still is idealized in the marriage of Lord Shiva and the Goddess Shakti. The sexual union of these two equal forces sustains the world and its people.

Continuing even today, worship of the Hindu God Shiva includes worship of the holy phallus. The ancient ritual of lingam (phallic) worship thrives in Shiva's temples, where natural phallic stones or carved images of the male organ are bathed, anointed, garlanded, and offered sacred foods such as rice. Corresponding to these religious acts, Hindu women wear the red bindi upon their foreheads not only to signify their marital or caste states but as a symbol of their sacred, sexual femininity or Shakti (Goddess) power. The crimson bindi signifies the moon and the third eye and, above all, the vagina in all its holiness.

Tribal cultures around the world know of the intense spiritual power that awakens in a young adult at puberty. At puberty, the pituitary and pineal glands are at their most active. When these glands release hormones, the dormant Kundalini energy at the base of the spine is also stimulated and cosmic awareness can be reached, sometimes without effort. Because of this release of sexual and spiritual energy, mystical rites of the tribe are held, thus giving the young person access into religious and social activities of the community.

Sometimes the energy release of an adolescent is so intense that it manifests as poltergeist phenomena. The teenage years often bring vivid dreams, visions, and insights that quickly dissolve when adult responsibilities are assumed in the busy, practical outside world.

Because of the intricate obligations of career, marriage, and family, most of us rarely experience the mystical but, when we do, it is most often during meaningful lovemaking. This is why sacred sexual expression is so important. Yes, love and sex are avenues to the Divine when we are with a like-minded partner. The beloved alone is our passage to spiritual completeness when we draw on the energy of unconditional love.

Many of us find it difficult to meld spirituality with sensuality due to societal conditioning. The issue of guilt is sometimes consuming, and we lock the wild, beautiful bird of our sexuality in a cage of inhibition, self-criticism, and shame. In reality, we are closest to God when we are expressing love. Sexual expression by itself is a one-sided experience that often leaves us hollow, so we seek it again and again in order to find the depth of ecstasy we all know is possible between two people. But sexuality with love is multi-dimensional and capable of erasing all shame from our consciousness with its purity.

While we are in the spirit body, this purity can be found without much struggle because in the invisible worlds we are more likely to meet someone who is of a like vibration or energy. When we exchange affection, love, and sexual desire in the soul body, we not only can match or surpass the greatest of physical lovemaking but we have an advantage. As soul travelers, we can experience something that can only be fully experienced between two souls, which is called melding.

When two spirits meld, each spirit exchanges energy with the other. In actuality, this act of giving and taking energy results in explosive ecstasy, consciousness expansion, orgasmic euphoria, and complete loss of identity. At its best, melding can take a soul directly into the consciousness of the Ultimate Deity. There are many types of meldings, including chakra meldings, spirit fusions, non-sexual meldings (with plants, animals, beings), and light body meldings.

You may be asking, "How do you meld?" Melding is an inborn ability of the soul and does not have to be learned, but the knowledge of fusing certain chakras greatly enhances the experience. Meldings can be planned or happen without warning when two like souls come in contact with one another. The melding experience differs with cosmic mates, astral lovers, et cetera. No melding is like another, so each time we fuse with a beloved being, the sensation also differs.

When we meld out of body and return to the physical, our bodily sexual needs and desires are completely fulfilled unless the experience was partial or with a sexually dominant energy or individual. Of course, the melding and lovemaking experience can be so spellbindingly orgasmic, it is possible that you will return to your body wanting more. The depth of sensation even reaches the physical body, and each cell is euphorically aware that it has been loved. This is the gift of each successful melding: the physical and spiritual knowledge that we are essentially instruments of divine love.

Meldings, when with a cosmic mate or a vibrationally harmonious astral lover, can go a step further than ecstasy and catalyze physical and emotional healing. When a melding begets transformation in our physical lives, we have reached the highest state of loving; we have moved beyond the emotion of love and harnessed the energy of love. Perhaps this is the ultimate goal of all lovers.

Though meldings involve the exchange of soul essence, it is possible to make love in the physical body and experience such fusion, though the experience is not as profound or visually apparent (physical melding will be discussed in depth in Chapter 10).

Because actual physical lovemaking is possible in the soul body, the most profound meldings occur when actual lovemaking takes place. Since the soul body retains every function, sensation, and characteristic of the earthly body, the full sexual experience in the spirit body is just as it is in the physical. Since this is closest to our experience as human beings, lovemaking will be discussed first, followed by in-depth melding procedures.

Physical Lovemaking in the Soul Body

Making love in the spirit body is wonderfully free because issues of birth control and disease are nonexistent. As soul travelers and lovers, we have the entire universe to experience. There are no boundaries, restrictions, or prying eyes.

My initiation into astral lovemaking took place during a morning sojourn. My lover and I were both out of body, and each light and shadow of that spring morning intoxicated our senses. A warm breath of wind blew across a lake fringed with bluegrass, and purple violets colored the surrounding fields not yet cut. Dorian gave me daffodils, and we made love for the first time in the cool bed of tall grasses. I did not expect to feel so deeply, physically or emotionally, because a part of me believed that making love in the spirit body would somehow be vague. I did not expect to experience orgasm, and the pleasure moved me to tears. I will never forget the feeling of oneness not only with Dorian but with the entire earth. We were dense like our physical forms, but when the wind blew across the lake, it blew through us. The earth beneath our joined bodies embraced us, and we felt an ancient divinity cradling us. We had not only made love to one another, but the earth had made love to us, too.

Though Dorian is not with me today, we occasionally see one another as kindred, old friends. No matter how many years pass, when I smell new grass on the winds and see a blue May sky, I am seventeen again.

From my experience through the years, astral lovemaking can be cosmic or it can be very grounded or playful. Just as physical sex has many moods and faces, astral sex is as diverse. But what would be inconvenient physically, such as making love in the sand or in a cold rainstorm, is hassle-free in the soul body. Also, if it is desired, continuous lovemaking is possible without recuperative periods for the male. As wonderful as this is, don't be surprised to find that you often choose the more mundane way of doing things because of the fact that you miss the physical, everyday experiences with your astral lover or cosmic mate. What other people take for granted or find annoying may actually be the things you feel deprived of. However, this is the beauty of astral life: If you don't feel like being obedient to the physical, you can always cheat!

Another advantage to astral lovemaking is the fact that you can make love in places where it would be difficult or impossible physically. I remember a time when my present partner and I discovered a remote and precipitous waterfall in the wilds of Hawaii. The grassy, moonlit banks bordering the water were too dangerous to approach in the physical, but effortless in the spirit body. Needless to say, we made love like we found lost Eden. Because the location was unapproachable, the energy was undiluted and magical, which gave our lovemaking a pristine yet almost primitive eroticism.

Lastly, when you make love astrally, it is possible for you to see the actual energy that you and your partner create. If you are with someone who is your vibrational equal, the energy will be even more visual. Many times after making love in a dark space, my lover and I have been startled to see hundreds of prismatic lights flashing like comets around us. Over time, I have noticed that when our lovemaking is deeply emotional and spiritual, we are encircled by breathtaking blue light that is stationary or slow moving; and if our time together is passionate and thunderous, the light is multi-colored, brilliant, and vigorous. During these moments, we often experience spontaneous meldings. Though meldings can occur at any time, they often occur during those moments after orgasm when both lovers are basking in the euphoria of pleasure and complete understanding. Like a magnet, without warning, lover and beloved fuse together in an explosion of light. At its best, a spontaneous melding such as this is almost frightening in intensity and electricity that is so ecstatic physically, emotionally, and spiritually, the previous lovemaking seems to be just a warm-up to the main event. The more in sync you are with your partner, the more intense and electrifying the melding will be.

The best way to take advantage of spontaneous melding is to remain in the position of lovemaking for a few long moments after orgasm. Especially if you are a heterosexual couple, remain interlocked.

This act of remaining enfolded, while both lovers are still pulsating and deeply communicating non-verbally, seems to spark a sudden, urgent melding. The length of the melding varies, sometimes being a few long seconds or, when it is exceptionally good, a few minutes. The sensation of being inside one another in a womb of vibrating light is indescribable and always breathtaking. It is like being one entity, one pulsing heart of fire. As fast as you meld, you also part. It still amazes me to see the light spark and peak like an enormous flame and then suddenly dissolve. It's like being in a brightly lit room and the lights unexpectedly go out.

Though spontaneous meldings are extremely rewarding, planned meldings are extraordinary as well. Let's look at the many possibilities.

Melding in the Soul Body

There is no right or wrong way to meld, but it is essential to completely surrender to what is happening or the experience will not be what it can be. Also, occasionally you may notice that melding is not as free-flowing as other times. This may be attributed to emotional blocks in the heart chakra due to withholding anger or tears. If you experience this awkwardness, make a point of releasing any suppressed feelings before melding. The usual ease will immediately return, and melding will be as wonderful as always.

The Fusion Melding

The fusion melding will probably be the first melding you will experience because it is the most commonly experienced. Anyone who has used watercolors on damp paper can understand the nature of the fusion melding. Just as two colors bleed into one another by the brush of an artist, two souls similarly blend into each other.

This type of melding can either be very energizing or peace-inducing but, in either case, you will feel as if you are dissolving into a dream. This feeling of dissolution into another being is actually your energy and another's energy becoming one energy.

The fusion melding can be either sexual in nature or non-sexual. If it is sexual, you will feel waves of unspeakable pleasure akin to a powerful full-body climax. If it is non-sexual, you will feel totally one with the other energy, as if you've been embraced from the inside out. The non-sexual fusion melding can be experienced with animals, plants, and any life form.

During my journeys, I often meet up with a beloved pet I had to leave behind because of a complicated relocation. Each time I embrace my four-legged angel, I feel the cat's energy enter my heart center. These non-sexual, pure meldings are poignant and warm, and they always remind me that the relationships we have with animals are the most spiritual. Experiencing a fusion melding with an animal can put you in touch with the universal rhythms for days.

To experience a fusion melding with any being or energy, simply allow your soul body to dissolve into the other's force field and allow the other energy to dissolve into you. It will initially feel like immersing yourself in warm sea water, that moment when you let go of the bottom and drift into the arms of the wave. Don't feel that you are losing a part of yourself that you cannot get back. At the conclusion of any melding, each soul energy involved will once again be independent and whole. During a fusion melding, emotional and spiritual responses are usually intense. You may laugh with euphoria or cry with joy. Allow all feelings to progress or the melding will be interrupted. The energy must continue to flow and be exchanged at all times in order for both parties to reach an ecstatic summit.

The Heart Melding

The heart melding usually occurs between two people deeply attached to one another either spiritually or emotionally. This melding can again be either sexual or non-sexual, but most of the time it is a little of both. In any case, this melding is by far the purest. Since the essence of the Ultimate Deity dwells within the heart chakra, the heart melding is an actual exchange of this God energy.

When you are engaged in this melding, you experience powerful love not only for the other being but for all of creation. You are able to love each and every speck of life on any plane as you would love an intimate partner and, in turn, you feel the universe embracing you with ardor. During the heart melding, you may feel as if your heart is going to burst, that you cannot take another moment of giving and receiving love of such magnitude. When you reach this point, don't turn away—surrender to the crushing ecstasy of the soul's embrace with the cosmos.

To experience the heart melding, stand face to face with your partner or with your back against the other's breast. Feel love for this being rise in your chest. As you do this, there will be a beautiful and sudden force pulling you together at heart level. It often feels as if you are a tiny leaf being washed away by furious, thrilling rapids.

If you wish to experience an even more emotional melding, fuse not only the heart chakras but the belly chakras as well. By melding this way, you are exchanging both God energy and your human emotions collected in the solar plexus. This results in a deeply powerful bond with the other being that will last long after the melding is concluded.

If you are a little uncertain about the mechanics of melding, rest assured that nature takes over. If you still find it confusing, simply imagine light shining from the chakra into your partner's corresponding center. This way, you can never go wrong.

The Cosmic Melding

The cosmic melding usually is reserved for coupling with an advanced being such as a cosmic mate, but if you and an astral lover are deeply, spiritually in love, this melding can also be ideal. This melding catapults you into direct communion with Deity and momentarily eclipses your identity and present consciousness. This loss of self in the beloved and in the All may sound intimidating or frightening but, when it is accomplished, the result is an unforgettable, even life-altering, spiritual experience. The true state of bliss or nirvana can be reached with the cosmic melding, but the only obstacle to success is when sexual desire is dominant. So to fully experience the true cosmic melding, choose a time when sexual fulfillment is not a driving need or motive for melding.

To experience a cosmic melding, stand face to face with your partner. For even better results, attempt this melding within the light-drenched realms of the third plane if possible. Imagine light beaming from your heart and crown chakras into your partner's corresponding centers as he or she follows suit simultaneously. The moment when both crown chakras merge, you will feel ignited with awesome force. As both of your beings unite in a solitary, blazing fire of energy, darts of light will spark away from you. For the first few moments you will feel power surge through you with pleasure beyond comprehension and then, all within a breath, you will find that your consciousness is completely drawn inward. When this drawing in occurs, you momentarily become unaware of your partner, your own thoughts, your own ecstasy. Suddenly you will only be. This loss of identity and awareness of time and matter will usher you into a state of bliss that you have never experienced in the physical body. You will feel completely inseparable from all of creation. Ultimately, you will understand that, above all else, God is essentially a state of being, a moment when you remember that you are everything and everything is you.

Before you and your partner divide naturally, you will feel your consciousness again emerging. You will feel as though a vacuum is sweeping you back into your identity. As this happens, you and your partner will probably experience a mutual orgasm that is felt in every particle of your spirit body. This sensual ecstasy can be intentionally prolonged by remaining together when you feel that you are going to part. When you resist the normal division of your bodies, this orgasmic state will not wane, but continue with steady power. However, from my own experience, I have found that prolonging the state often has a draining effect on you. This means that the energy you created and received from the melding is now counteracting because, in order to maintain the orgasmic summit, energy is being used instead of being generated. So if you want to come out of it with tremendous vitality, allow the melding to conclude when it naturally wants to. You can always repeat the melding to experience more, and this way you will not be drained.

The Lover's Melding

Even though there are many ways to meld with the chakras, the lover's melding can be the most intoxicating and erotic.

Since the lover's melding is so sexually intense and emotionally charged, if engaged in too often, you can return to your physical body feeling like a wet blanket. The sexual force can be the most healing of forces but, when mishandled, it can also be the most depleting of forces. Also, when sexually intense meldings are engaged in too often, the Kundalini energy may stay locked in the lower chakras, which can result in the inability to travel to finer spiritual realms or experience spiritual ecstasy during other meldings. So indulge—but save some for next week!

To experience the lover's melding, face your partner and imagine light beaming from the root chakra, belly chakra, and the heart chakra into your partner's corresponding effort. The fusion of the root and belly centers gives the melding a deep sexual nature while the unity of the heart centers intensifies the experience with pure love energy.

As you meld, it will probably be urgent, and you will both explode into climax immediately. You can experience this sexual ecstasy for an extended time, but even a taste of the lover's melding goes a long way. Just a few long seconds of melding this way gives you sexual satisfaction that is found in hours of usual lovemaking.

For an exciting twist, try this melding during astral lovemaking. Sanschi and I once soared into a flaming blue twilight and made love in the cool embrace of the wind. At the moment of climax, we used the lover's melding. As we drifted over snow-crowned mountains, we experienced the most exhilarating, intoxicating, and erotic time ever spent together. Use your imagination—be daring and creative! Add the lover's melding to your amorous activity and it will be unforgettable.

The Light Body Melding

The light body melding is the most powerful of all meldings but in order for it to be a complete success, your partner must be a cosmic mate or a very emotionally and spiritually intimate astral lover.

As stated in Chapter 5, one can only enter the higher spiritual realms in the vehicle of a refined light body. When other techniques fail, using the light body melding with the appropriate partner can make it possible.

Going into a light body erases all of your characteristics and, for a while, you are only consciousness in the form of silver or golden light. When you become a light form with a beloved, you are able to travel to unknown worlds together. But in order to accomplish becoming light energy, this melding must be done within the inner planes above the earth plane, preferably within the third or fourth.

While you are within the third or fourth plane, face your partner and press your palms together. Beginning at the root chakra, imagine light beaming from the first center into your partner's as he or she does the same. When you are joined at the root chakra, you will feel incredible sexual desire that you must use. Instead of getting lost in the lust of the moment (which is totally natural to want to do), both of you must imagine this energy rising upward through the rest of your chakras. When you will this sexual energy upward, you are actually raising the Kundalini energy. Instead of stimulating only your own Kundalini, since you are fused you are sharing this energy as one being. As each pair of chakras meld, it will be an electrifying sensation due to the fast-rising current of psychic fire on its way to the crown centers. Once this current reaches the tops of both your heads, you will see a blinding silver-white light and, in a breath of a second, you will become two individual light bodies. You will have no limbs, no features, because you will be a pulsating sphere of exquisite light. Though you are in the simplest form you can be in, you will retain all of your senses.

When you become a light form, you will probably have a cellular memory of being in this state before you had a physical body. You are simply returning to your soul's natural state of naked fire, which is the true, immortal, ever-knowing nucleus of the being you are.

Though this melding can be very easy when attempted with a cosmic mate, it may take a few tries to accomplish the transformation with an astral lover. As you practice it, forget the goal of becoming a light body and enjoy the most cosmic of all meldings. NOTE: During your light body melding, you may notice additional chakra centers that exceed the usually known seven. You may find these deeply hidden centers only during an intense melding such as this one because they are sufficiently stimulated. You may discover a center between the solar plexus and heart chakras, a center between the heart and throat chakras, and powerful centers in the palms of your hands.

The Healer's Melding

The healer's melding can stimulate healing and transformation on any level if you are in need of it. Though the most successful of healing meldings are those with a cosmic mate, if you and your astral lover are deeply in love, wonderful results are possible. This melding can also be done with three beings, but works best when only two do it. If you have a same-sex partner, platonic or intimate, this melding will work with amazing effects. No matter who your partner is, be very sure that he or she is honest and not an energy-draining being.

To be the channeler in the healer's melding, imagine light energy beaming from your heart chakra into your partner's troubled area, such as the leg, stomach, or throat. Wherever the problem is in the physical body, direct your light energy to that place. If your partner has an emotional or mental issue, direct your heart force into his or her heart center. Heart-to-heart meldings are the most powerful and beneficial for the healing of past trauma, grief, fear, and anger.

For best results, this melding should take place on a regular basis until the desired results begin to manifest on the physical plane. Also, to prevent the channeler from being drained of his or her energy, one should not will the light energy outward but simply allow the heart force to travel to the place of need. The heart energy is independent of personal will and therefore does not need the personal power of the channeler to stimulate results. In order to do this, the channeler should leave all will, ego, desire, and identity out of the healing direction as much as possible. In turn, the receiving partner should totally surrender to the love being sent. Both partners will experience deep warmth, bonding, and joy with this melding. It is the most tender of all cosmic embraces.

The Energy Direction Melding

This melding allows you and your partner to direct energy into the invisible worlds in order to manifest a result on the physical plane.

While you are in the soul body with a like-minded partner, concentrate on a need or desire you wish to manifest. Both of you should focus on the same goal at the same time. As you are doing this, face one another and imagine light beaming into each other's brow chakras. When your brow chakra melds with your partner's, you will feel and see a tremendous light emanate from your foreheads. While this beautiful white or purple light is extending outward, imagine the need or desire leaving your thoughts through the light and reaching the earth plane. If your visualization is strong and your melding is joyful, you will eventually see results, though you may have to do this many times in order to build the psychic energy necessary for physical manifestation.

The sensation of this melding is one of strength. You will feel in charge of your destiny, physically and mentally powerful. During this melding, a current of happiness surges up your spine that is spiritual rather than sensual, and you will feel charged with cosmic force.

The Group Melding

A group melding involves three or more beings and is almost always non-sexual in the sense that the orgasmic state is of spiritual ecstasy rather than sensual. Group meldings can be brilliant fusions that give each soul body added energy, psychic stimulation, or inspiration. In order to be memorable, group meldings should only be done with like-minded individuals.

I have been in group meldings of three as well as more than twenty. Because we all had similar passions involving creativity and spirituality, I came away from these meldings with renewed vitality.

To experience a group melding, stand with your partners in a circular gathering and hold hands. Choose one individual who will begin by extending his or her aura outward as far as possible. The moment one being's force field reaches the one beside him or her, the rest will catch fire, so to speak. This is the most fascinating of meldings because light energy travels through each individual aura like wildfire. The result is a blazing triangle (if there are three of you) or circle (if there are four or more of you) of psychic energy. You will feel euphoria, ecstasy, and completely at one with each member of the melding party. It is like being part of a spiritual army that acts and feels like one massive individual consciousness. Group meldings can be ideal for sending healing energy to someone apart from the group or for physical manifestation, like the energy direction melding.

Whether you begin your own secret spiritual society or join one already in progress, the group melding is an experience of cosmic kinship that will bring you love, acceptance, and needed change.

No matter which type of meldings you experience and discover, you will witness love in its purest state—energy. And once its impenetrable mystery is glimpsed, you will ultimately realize that we are all love—love manifested—and nothing less.

Chapter Nine

Same-Sex Lovers

Brothers of Apollo,

Sisters of Sappho

Among ancient cultures around the world, the Greek civilization praised homoerotic love perhaps more than any other culture. From the mythical loves and losses of the god Apollo to the alleged lesbian poetess Sappho, no race has portrayed same-sex relationships as beautifully or as positively as the Greeks.

Love fought against, feared, finally accepted;
Love no better than Her other gowns . . .
Love that adorns, adorns me tonight.

During the golden age of Greek philosophy, male homosexuality was considered to be holy, while traditional marriage was looked on as lower, for practical convenience and continuation of the bloodline only. Males of all ages left their homes to meet with other males for lively discussion of the arts and sciences as well as for erotic pleasure. Though lesbianism was considered to be a shameful practice in the male-dominated period of the classical Greeks, the rites of Demeter and Persephone secretly encouraged the sexual and non-sexual bonding between female celebrants.

Among various tribal cultures, the shaman often is and was homosexual. Within these tribes, the homosexual is considered to have the calling for shamanic office not only because of his artistic and mystical gifts but because of the absence of familial obligations that can prevent the shaman from reaching full spiritual power.

Throughout history, homoeroticism has had deep roots in spirituality, ritual, and the arts. From artistic genius Michelangelo to famed writer-poet May Sarton, many creative men and women have found their muse in the same sex.

Today, many gay people are finding spiritual acceptance in alternative religions, as well as rediscovering their mystical selves in sacred sexuality. In her groundbreaking book *Another Mother Tongue,* lesbian poet-author Judy Grahn discusses the spiritual and psychic experiences of the same-sex couple during lovemaking. The author recounts the events of her consciousness projections as well as her ability to see spirit lights before and after orgasm.

Homosexuality within the inner worlds is not a target for moral judgment but a natural occurrence. During one of my journeys, I met a young man who had been homosexual in his physical body and who was, at least for the time being, still gay. I asked him, from his new spiritual knowledge since his death, what the karmic purpose of homosexuality is. He said that the main purpose of homosexuality on the earth plane is to spread global tolerance throughout our race. Aside from this very simple but difficult duty, homosexuality can be a channel for emotional and spiritual healing as well.

Melding with a same-sex partner in the spirit realms can be exactly like heterosexual melding experiences, but the polarity balance can differ. Spiritual power and energy is most easily generated by the union of opposites, very much like magnetism. Up until the fifth plane, energy and balance are birthed from the yin/yang principle, male and female, light and dark, et cetera. To experience supreme meldings, a same-sex couple should touch on this harmony of polarity.

Each of us carries the characteristics of both sexes as well as an inner opposite sex that Jung called the animus (inner male) and the anima (inner female). Using this inner personality, both partners of a same-sex relationship can awaken their opposite energy before making love or melding. By doing this, a complete balance is created; therefore, the couple is charged, so to speak. This spiritual charging is the beginning of wonderful cosmic experiences.

To stimulate your inner opposite, while in the soul body and before melding or making love, take a few moments to center yourself. Imagine your exact twin but of the opposite sex. What would he or she look like? See features, coloring, and personality in your mind's eye. Hear the speaking voice of your twin. Imagine every aspect of your counterpart. Some people who do this visualization actually see visions and images of their opposite twin, so if you see him or her, know that it is natural.

Once you feel that you know this extension of yourself, place both hands over the root and belly chakras if you are a woman. Proceed to stimulate or open these centers by moving your hands in a clockwise direction while imagining light beaming from your palms into the chakras. Stimulate one chakra at a time until you feel warmth or a sensation of expansion, which is the signal that the center is opening. Women should focus on the two lower chakras for polarity balance because these centers are vibrationally akin to the yang, or male, universal energy.

If you are a man, after you visualize your inner female, place both hands over the throat and brow chakras. Proceed to stimulate these centers by moving your hands in a clockwise direction while imagining light beaming from your palms into the chakras. Stimulate each center until you feel warmth or a sensation of expansion, which means that these centers are opening. Men should focus on these chakras because they are vibrationally akin to the yin, or female, universal energy.

The remaining major chakras—the solar plexus, heart, and crown—all carry an equal balance of both yin and yang energy. Anyone of any sexual preference can benefit by polarity balancing.

Like heterosexual melding, same-sex melding can either be sexual or non-sexual. Of either nature, the same-sex melding can be a powerful tool for healing, especially emotional. During a challenging time, Sanschi and I melded with an advanced female being. When my energy melded with her yin energy, I experienced great spiritual peace and emotional well-being that reached even my physical consciousness. Melding with anyone of the same sex is a beautiful experience because any shared emotion or inspiration is intensified due to like energies. This unspoken understanding channels such vibrational purity that deep healing is possible.

No matter who we love, fall in love with, or make love with, we are all empty vessels until we are filled with love and we in turn fill someone else's empty vessel. This is our most important task as spiritual beings.

In our modern society, pure love is an endangered resource. If we are lucky enough to find it and share it, we have not lived in vain. If you have found this gift with someone of the same sex, your single life can illumine the ignorance of this world the same way a single candle can light a thousand. If you are someone who has difficulty in accepting this square in love's immense, many-colored quilt, try to remember that we are all worthy of love. The Ultimate Deity knows no gender and neither does the sun that we travel around. We have been male and female many times in the course of our spiritual evolution; before we chose to wear any physical body, we were genderless energy. Essentially, when we truly love another person, we love the original being beneath the cloak of flesh.

Loving another person is the most important thing you will ever accomplish in any body, on any plane, so let's all love and let love.

Chapter Ten

Winged Sandals

Soul-Sex in the

Physical Body

*P*hysical lovemaking and spiritual enlightenment have gone hand in hand in Eastern religious teachings since ancient times. This philosophy, called Tantric Yoga, has been practiced for thousands of years to attain Nirvana. Though these Tantric teachings are beautiful, mystical, and very useful, many couples find the techniques to be too complex, rigid, cryptic, or time consuming.

Breath rising, brown hair blows into black.
We merge, hearts drumming . . .
Scarlet of passion and blue of soul;
Violet unity.

Physical lovemaking with or without Tantric discipline can be an avenue to psychic awakening, soul travel, and deep mystical experience. The following lovemaking rituals are specially designed for heterosexual or same-sex couples on the physical plane, but can easily be adapted to spirit couples. I've chosen and designed these rituals to parallel ancient customs of worship and those that honor the inner divinity and Deity in each of us. I will explain the background for these sensual ceremonies a little later.

In our modern world, views on sexuality are broadening to such an extent that the lines that used to divide and define our sexual behavior are almost erased. In this age of sensual freedom that declares "anything goes and everything's okay," inhibition has been unchained but unfortunately has created an emotional chasm between the lover and the beloved. As a society, we have become satisfied with the brief fulfillment of the moment, which has inspired us to build relationships from a foundation of sexual desire. In the mad rush to find ecstasy, we have forgotten that true sexual beauty and passion are the by-products of partnerships based on love and emotional grace.

Twenty-four hours a day, we are bombarded with outside influences telling us that we're not good lovers unless we fantasize, use sex toys, or consider sex to be a sport. These things may be fine in the proper place at the proper time, but all of these divide two lovers. In order to rediscover Eden, we have to cut through all of these distracting layers and again find the true essence of the beloved. Beneath sexual experimentation, novelties, and hollow trends, there is a naked soul and a beating heart of the lover, and it can only be found when we remember that making love is a gift. It is a gift to have a body that can be an instrument of love. It is a gift to bless another human being with ecstasy. It is a gift to know another person as only a lover can.

When we stand naked in front of another human being, we are giving all that we came into this life with and the only thing we truly own until death—the body, the temple of the soul. We would not enter a place of worship with selfish motivation or momentary lust for gratification. We would not dirty the purity of a place of holiness with disrespect or dishonor, or enter with a false heart. Yet we do these things to our lovers and allow our lovers to do the same to us. In our age of disease, promiscuity, and isolation, we must once again see the body as a sacred instrument, a holy place, and a gift not to be given in a moment's carelessness.

This certainly does not mean that making love has to be conservative, serious, rigid, or sober. On the contrary, this means that we should make love with the trust, honesty, and wonder of children. The bottom line is to again find mirth and play and love with all of our strength, to rediscover the joy of a smile, the beauty of eyes that love you, the bliss of warm arms in the night, and the ecstasy of shared pleasure that is found only in the mere presence of that special someone.

We don't need fantasy because love can be a reality. We don't need artificial sexual stimulants because the lover has all the things that are necessary to take us to the moon with fulfillment. It is like the true perfume of the rose—it cannot be simulated, duplicated, or substituted. But before we can be ready for the true, undiluted beloved, we have to stop being satisfied with replacements.

Sex without soul is like food without flavor; it can keep us going but our spirits starve. So you may feel the same way but you may be in a relationship that has lost luster. Or you think that you can go deeper with your partner but you're afraid to rock the boat. In either case, ritual is an ideal medium to bring you and your lover to euphoric heights. Ritual transforms the mundane into the exotic or mystical as well as reuniting the physical with the spiritual while leaving room for playfulness and erotic excitement.

The following rituals mirror ancient customs of worship from cultures such as the Greeks and Hindus. All of them are designed to encourage the inner lover to find its way back to the wilderness of its own spirit. And a few are intended just to inspire creativity and fun. Feel free to add or take away elements, create your own, or combine the rituals.

The Ambrosia Ritual

What you will need:

- ¼ cup pure evaporated sea salt (available at health food stores)
- Pure rose water (available at health food or culinary shops)
- Pure essential oil (myrrh, lavender, or gardenia)
- Candles
- Pure incense (rose, jasmine, or gardenia)
- Pure massage oil (floral or spice; available at health food or natural body shops)
- Fresh fruits, washed, peeled, and sliced (suggestions: orange and honey, mango and peach, or honeydew melon and kiwi)
- Music (suggestions: *Watermark* by Enya [soulful, mystical]; *India* by Kitaro [exotic, hypnotic]; *Timeless Motion* by Daniel Kobialka [quiet, shimmering]; *Toward the Within* by Dead Can Dance [Live vocal—exotic, powerful])

The ancient worship of the Greek goddess of love, Aphrodite, included an annual procession to the sea. An image of the goddess was ritually bathed in the surf, signifying her original birth from sea foam. After the ceremonial cleansing, the image was then anointed with costly perfumes and garlanded with fragrant flowers.

As a ritual preparation, bathe in water containing a quarter cup of pure evaporated sea salt, a few capfuls of pure rose water, and a few drops of essential oil. Be sure to bathe alone and have your lover do the same. This should be an inviolate time of solitude when, in the sanctity of your own thoughts, you are awakening the spiritual being within.

As you bathe, visualize washing away any unwanted emotions, memories, or fears. Know that you are being reborn in this womb of salted, fragrant water like Aphrodite. If you are a man, you may wish to concentrate on the power and sensuality of the Greek God of the Sea, Poseidon.

When you step out of the water, feel the inner Deity emerge as well. You may wish to remain unclothed or dress in exotic or luxurious garments. Remember that both you *and* your divine self are greeting your partner.

After you both have bathed separately, you may wish to construct an altar, a holy corner where candles and incense can be burned in honor of the divinities within and without. Feel free to sprinkle the floor or bed with flowers. Be creative—for the next hour or hours, this will be your temple. Play your chosen music and be sure the CD, tape, or record can continuously play if you wish. Finally, place the bowl of succulent fruit near the area where you will make love.

Face your partner and take turns giving the other a blessing by kissing each part of the other's body, beginning at the head. As you do this, thank the other person for what they have given you or others. For example, kiss your lover's forehead and thank him or her for their intelligence, their lips for their words of encouragement and expressions of love, et cetera.

After you bless one another, spend at least a minute deep breathing and looking into each other's eyes. Inhale together. Exhale together. When you are both ready, say, one to the other, "Today (tonight) I give you my heart, relinquishing all fear of tomorrow. Today I give you my trust, discarding all doubt. Today I give you my dreams, so they may nourish your hungry hours. Today I give you my faith, so I may know God with you. Today I give you my love, so

177

I may be a better person by loving you. Today I give you my body, so it may be an instrument of my love. Today I give you all the selves I have been, the self I am now, and the selves I will be tomorrow."

After you both express these words, take turns anointing each other with a sensual but pure massage oil. As you anoint your lover, anoint the god or goddess within your lover. Totally surrender to this sacred offering of touch, making sure you leave no area of the body unsavored and unrecognized. Take this opportunity to know and revere every muscle, bone, and dimple, paying special attention to your favorite places. Take a slow journey through the landscape of your lover.

At the end of your anointing, take a small amount of fruit and feed it to your partner, imagining it is sacred ambrosia, the mythical fare of the gods and immortality. After you both have been anointed and fed by the other, allow the natural course of lovemaking to follow.

When you feel the pleasure is reaching a summit before orgasm, visualize the physical ecstasy rising upward toward the top of your head. Put all of the power, all of the pleasure into this effort to raise the Kundalini that has already been awakened through sexual stimulation. If you are successful (practice will make you successful), you will have a cosmic or mystical experience during or shortly after climax.

Feel free to end the ritual whenever or however you wish.

The Lotus Ritual

What you will need:

- Pure orange flower water or jasmine water (available at health food, culinary, or natural body shops)
- Pure essential oil (sandalwood, patchouli, or ylang ylang)

- Candles

- Pure incense (sandalwood, patchouli, or saffron)

- Sensuous fabrics or sheets

- Music (suggestions: *Passion* by Peter Gabriel [exotic, ethnic, sensual]; *Bolero* by Ravel [hypnotic, progressive, passionate]; *Indian Ragas* by Ravi Shankar [traditional, sensuous]; any percussion work, especially by Mickey Hart; any Hindustani flute music)

Bhakti Yoga, the Hindu Path of Devotion, is based on complete adoration of Deity. Krishna—the Supreme Avatar and mystical lover from Indian scripture and myth—is passionately worshiped with joyous dancing, music making, chanting and singing, and adornment. These sacred practices bring the devotee into direct communion with the Supreme Godhead, resulting in salvation.

Also within the Hindu tradition, Shiva, lord of creation, destruction, and the universe, is represented by the holy lingam, or phallus. Phallic images are anointed and revered as symbols of fertility, prosperity, and power.

To bring these ancient elements into your intimate moments, bathe in water that is fragranced with pure essential oils and a few capfuls of orange flower or jasmine water. Bathe alone because this is your sacred time before approaching your lover and the Ultimate Deity. As you bathe, imagine that you are in the sunlit waters of the Ganges, India's holiest river. Visualize all impurities of mind and body dissolving into the sacred waves. If you are a woman, you may wish to imagine your inner goddess as the Hindu goddess of creativity and the river Ganges, Saraswati, or the all-empowering consort of Shiva, the goddess Shakti. If you are a man, you may wish to invoke your inner god akin to Lord Shiva, whose phallus is all-creating.

When you emerge from the water, feel the power of your own divinity. You may remain unclothed or dress in sensuous, exotic robes or fabrics. If you are a woman, before greeting your partner, apply a *bindi* (red spot of power) between the brows (lipstick is easiest to remove). The bindi signifies your divine feminine power, goddess energy, and the sacredness of your vagina and womb. If you are a man, anoint your own phallus with a drop or two of pure sandalwood or patchouli essential oil while you focus on the power of your inner god.

Light candles and drape beautiful fabrics or sheets on the floor or bed. You may even wish to create a canopy with the fabrics by hanging them from the ceiling or beams with push pins. Light the incense and play your chosen music. Be creative and erotic in your decoration. For the next few hours or so, this space is your altar, and your pleasure is an offering to the Supreme.

Face your partner with your hands in prayer position, close to your heart. Look into each other's eyes for at least a minute, then bow to one another as a symbol of peace, reverence, and greeting.

Sit across from each other and press the palms of your hands together. Slowly begin moving your hands in circles, making sure that each hand is moving in an opposite direction, one clockwise, the other counterclockwise. Begin to deep breathe. Inhale together. Exhale together. As your hands circle at a comfortable speed, focus on the cosmic union of Shiva and Shakti. Visualize their actual lovemaking, which is believed to sustain the cosmos. Feel that you are Shiva or Shakti. If you are a heterosexual couple, imagine that neither of you could exist without the other's opposite but equal energy. If you are a homosexual couple, imagine that neither of you could exist without the other's inner, opposite energy.

When you feel power rising between the two of you, stand up while sustaining your hand circles. Feel the energy building as your hands circle faster and faster. Focus on the music playing and begin to move to it. Listen to the music with your entire body, not only your ears. Dance away all inhibition, inviting pleasure and sensual movement. When it is a natural time, part your hands and just dance; dance for the Ultimate Deity and the divinity in each other. Smile, laugh, sigh, yell for joy. Do whatever comes naturally and comfortably.

Move closer to your partner until your movements are in sync. Move, dance, feel as one body, one sacred force. Kiss slowly and then move into a deeper kiss. Begin to make love and be consciously aware that it is a dance, the ultimate dance of beauty and joy. If you wish to, you may make love in the traditional Tantric position of the male sitting on the floor or a chair with the woman astride his lap.

As you make love, try to match your rhythm to the music until it becomes an unconscious impulse. Feel the music inside your body until you are both two rivers rising and falling to the heartbeat of the universe. As you approach orgasm, visualize the pleasure as fire that is rising through your entire body to the top of your head. Imagine the Kundalini energy moving upward as the ecstasy engulfs you. During or shortly after climax you may have a cosmic or mystical experience that brings you into a shared state of spiritual bliss. Practice will make you successful if it doesn't happen the first time.

Feel free to end the ritual whenever and however you wish.

The Melding Ritual

What you will need:

- Time (no less than two hours)

- Dried yarrow flowers (available at health food stores or herbal suppliers; to be made into a strong tea for bath water)

- Two cups pure spring water

- A dark room or a space drenched with sunlight

- Music (suggestions: *Fragrances of a Dream* by Daniel Kobialka [progressive, heartfelt]; *Somewhere in Time* soundtrack by John Barry [beautiful, haunting]; any recordings of Tibetan bells; any recordings of Gregorian chants; *Love's Illusion* by The Anonymous Four [feminine, angelic]; *The Scarlet Letter* soundtrack by John Barry [unforgettably beautiful, intimate])

This ritual simulates an astral melding experience. Though the results are not entirely like a true spirit melding, there will be a breathless experience of fusing body and soul with your lover.

To begin, simmer two handfuls of dried yarrow flowers in two cups of pure spring water for ten minutes. When the infusion is delicately colored with the herbs, strain the mixture and pour the hot or warm liquid into plain bath water. Each of you should make a separate infusion of yarrow and bathe alone. This should be a time of peace, when the mystical properties of the herbs are working with your natural energy field. Yarrow has long been used to stimulate the psychic centers, so be sure to wet the area between your brows with the bath water to awaken the psychic chakra.

As you bathe, imagine all of the day's concerns washing away, layer by layer, worry by worry. Feel clean in spirit as well as body. Feel spiritually powerful. When you emerge from your bath, don't dry yourself completely. Instead, allow your skin to be slightly damp so the magical vibration of the yarrow remains active.

A dark room or a room brightly lit and warmed by the sun is ideal for this ritual because in order for it to be successful, either light or the absence of it is very important. Moonlight and the sapphire hue of twilight are also perfect. Whatever you choose, be sure the room it comfortable, not too cool or too warm. Play your chosen music softly in the background.

Sit across from your lover and allow yourself to just be in his or her company. When you both reach a state of serene contentment without verbal communication, move into a slow, quiet embrace. For maximum comfort and spiritual closeness, you can sit astride your lover or your lover astride you while you both remain in a seated position. Embrace deeply, breathing in unison. As you inhale and exhale, embrace the other with all of your being. Imagine that you are a river emptying its entirety into the arms of the sea. Fill and be filled, using synchronized breathing as your guide. Have nothing of the outside world trespass into your thoughts. Pretend that nothing exists but the heartbeat of your beloved.

When you are both ready, progress into a deep kiss, holding the kiss for as long as you can. Become the kiss. Feel that you and your partner are melting into one another. Rediscover the sacredness of deep, languid kissing. Kissing can be the most spiritual of all sexual expression if both lovers see it as a soulful exchange rather than a warm-up to intercourse. If both lovers become the kiss, a change in consciousness will take place. Often the emotional and spiritual intimacy of this act reaches such an extraordinary summit that women experience orgasm without even being touched. So strive to take as much time as possible tasting each other's soul before proceeding with lovemaking. Make it a sacred offering.

When the time is right, make love like you will never make love again. Take each moment and each movement as slowly as possible. Leave room for silence, stillness. When you feel your head spinning with desire, take a minute to savor every sensation. After you slow down, something unexpected and beautiful happens—all of your senses reach a state of such extraordinary awareness that you feel like you were never alive before this moment. Allow yourself to be reborn through your lover's touch. Give birth to each other.

As you make love, move as one person. Forget your separateness and gender. Dance, breathe, and drown in the ecstasy of the realization that your souls are merging into one being. Feel every pulse and nuance of your partner's climax as if it were your own. If you are both in the same state of consciousness, there is a possibility that you will actually experience your lover's summit of pleasure separate from your own.

After orgasm, immediately embrace heart to heart and allow the energy to pass between you. Imagine that you are dissolving into one another. Feel that you are inside one another, enveloped within a womb of being. Allow love to pass through you like the wind through hollow reeds. At this point you may actually feel a cellular fusion or see light around the other person. Even if you only feel a deep, unspeakable intimacy, your auras are fused and your spirits have become one shimmering being on an invisible level.

Feel free to end the ritual whenever and however you wish to.

The Elemental Ritual

What you will need:

- Something to represent the earth (flowers, fresh pine boughs)

- Something to represent water (a small bowl of water, snow, or rose water)

- Something to represent fire (yellow, orange, or red candles)

- Something to represent air (pure incense)

This ritual, unlike the others, has an open format for your own choices. It simply recognizes elemental forces within nature and within your lover's body.

Before making love, construct a spiritual altar in the same room. Light candles for fire. Present an offering of water or rose water sprinkled with flower petals to the Invisibles. Burn incense to invoke the energies of the air. Drape the altar with fresh evergreen or bouquets of summer wildflowers. Be creative and honor the natural forces we take for granted every day.

Ancient cultures, including tribal nations, have acknowledged and revered earth, air, fire, and water in all aspects of daily living. Oriental Ayurvedic medicine takes it a step further and is a complete mind/body/spirit healing system based on human correspondence to the elements. So, as you decorate your lovemaking space, you too are participating in this age-old tradition of honoring nature in all her brilliance.

When you touch the body of your beloved, remember that bone, blood, and muscle mirror the density, power, and fertility of the earth. Touch your partner and touch the earth element within him or her. As you make love to your partner, think of warm, sunlit fields and tilling a garden when the earth smells like spring. Cultivate their pleasure and harvest their ecstasy.

When you kiss and taste your beloved, remember that tears, saliva, and sexual secretions reflect the rains, rivers, and seas. Drown yourself in the nectar of your loved one as your loved one becomes immersed in you. As you make love to your partner, think of rain pools and passionate surf. Drift and dream on the waves of their desire.

When you feel your beloved's breath, honor the winds and the air. Soar in the heaven of your lover's sighs.

When you feel spellbound by your beloved's fire, allow your entire being to dance like flames in the wind or find the calm, burning center of passion that can be still as a taper on a winter night. When you make love with your partner, honor the most mysterious element of all, fire.

Feel free to add anything to this ritual and to end it as you wish.

The Free Spirit Ritual

What you will need:

- Face/body paints, lipsticks, eyeliner pencils
- An hour or two of total abandon

This ritual also has no format, but is designed to bring out the inner child and the untamed nature within your lover's soul. Simply find a shred of madness in the moment and paint your lover's body like a canvas. Go ahead, be silly, erotic, and crazy—it'll be the most sensuous thing you've ever experienced. See through the eyes of an artist and transform breasts into daisies, bellies into suns, and thighs into falling stars. Have your lover close their eyes as you trace a wet sable brush over their body and turn your favorite canvas into a work of art.

Needless to say, if you allow inspiration to set all inhibitions free, eroticism with soulfulness could hit an all-time high. There is nothing closer to God than a shining hour of pure joy, so have fun and be enlightened, too!

The more you experience lover's rituals, you may find yourself seriously pursuing the spiritual art of Tantric Yoga or creating wonderful and ecstatic ceremonies. No matter how hectic your life is, try to reserve one day or a few hours every month just to reconnect with your beloved and the powers that be.

The Future of Love

Judging from my own observations of the other worlds, the love we share with someone on the earth plane is always continued in the next realm if this is what we want.

Two spirits, once reunited, may not remain together eternally, but a second chance always awaits us. Because love in the afterlife is not burdened with earthly complications, after death we are free to love and be loved more deeply than we could while living.

My soul walks with your soul.
Lost long, long lost, I reach love's earning.
As moon presses upon wave,
I am pressed to you . . .
Breathless, deathless in love's learning.

No matter how we suffer at the loss of a spouse or lover for any earthly reason, we will have a chance to make it right and see them again in the next life. No one is ever lost to us, even if they are reincarnated. Someday we will see them again as we have loved them. Love, like the soul, is our greatest teacher and is infinite energy. Beyond earthly love's briefness, loss, and frustration, love lives on. What a beautiful thing to look forward to! For every regret, there is another opportunity. For every loss, there is a second time with a loved one. For every unfulfillment, there is fruition.

As soul travelers, we are given a rare opportunity to see the possibilities of all reality. We are given a shining glimpse of the Universal Plan and blessed with the beautiful realization that all we are and all that we see is love manifested.

As lovers, we are given the chance to see ourselves and our loved ones as divine beings in the making, like spiritual clay on the potter's wheel of experience. Love molds us and dissolves us, only to begin again until we are sculpted into perfect vessels worthy to hold her roses. As the moon leaves its breath upon the waters, love leaves her mark on us, and we leave our mark on life until the soul directs its sails homeward.

In the meantime, love and be loved. This is all that is asked of us. If you have any experiences you'd like to share with me, I'd like to hear from you.

I wish you love.

Fledgling soul, take thy wings . . .

Search the earth to talk with kings.

Claim thy virgin star on high;

Uplift all life's stones.

Drink thy well of desire dry,

Then fly home, old soul, fly home.

Winifred M. Druhan

Akashic Records. An etheric library that holds vibrational records of all lives, thoughts, events, et cetera.

Astral Lovemaking. Sexual activity engaged in while out of body.

Astral Lover. A spirit of any plane who is a soul traveler's lover, companion, or mate.

Astral Parallel. Etheric counterpart of the planet earth or universe; the vibrational reality of the physical world.

Astral Plane. Common term for any plane of existence beyond the physical, manifested world.

Aura. The vibrational force field of a person, spirit, animal, plant, or object that serves as a protective shield of psychic forces; seen as prismatic light.

Chakra. One of the seven etheric energy centers of the physical and spiritual bodies; can be used as a gateway to leave the physical body and travel in the soul body.

Cosmic Consciousness. A state of consciousness when one remembers his or her Divine Self, which is connected to all of creation and the Ultimate Deity; can result in ecstatic visions, insights, and mystical experiences and is commonly the ultimate goal of a spiritual seeker.

Cosmic Mate. An advanced spirit who is a person's counterpart and vibrational equal; the ultimate spiritual mate.

Consciousness Projection. The projection of one's mind to a distant place; also called remote viewing.

Elemental. Common term for any spirit of earth, air, fire, or water.

Elemental Guide. An elemental that is a soul guide (see Soul Guide).

Higher Self. The all-knowing spiritual aspect of an individual that is linked to the Ultimate Deity

Human Double. The visible spirit of a living person; commonly called doppelgängar ("double-walker").

Incubus. A male entity from the lower astral realms that feeds off human sexual energy (see Succubus).

Karma. Eastern religious belief that one's actions determine future experiences and lives; the positive or negative result or reaction from past deeds.

Kundalini. Inherent spiritual force or "serpent fire" that sleeps at the base of the spine until activated; travels upward through each chakra until it reaches the crown. This results in cosmic consciousness (see Chakra, Cosmic Consciousness).

Light Body. A form of the soul/spirit that travels to higher spiritual planes of existence.

Lingam. Tantric term for the penis (see Yoni).

Lower Astral. Etheric realm of emotion and negativity; also etheric planes collectively called the hell world.

Melding. The fusion of two soul bodies and the exchange of energy that results in emotional, spiritual, and sexual ecstasy.

Mystic. An individual who strives to have direct communion with Deity; one who experiences visions, insights, out-of-body travel, and ecstatic states.

Planetary Rulers. Spirits who guard the planets.

Polarity Balancing. Balancing the male/female energies within the physical or spiritual body.

Power Animal. A guiding spirit in the form of an animal that guides, instructs, and protects a person or shaman.

Remote Viewing. Viewing distant places and people with the mind; projection of consciousness to a distant place.

Reincarnation. The transference of the soul into another physical form after bodily death.

Shaman. A person of either sex, usually of a tribal culture, who is the spiritual leader of the community; one who enters ecstatic states and interacts with the spirit world.

Silver Cord. The etheric thread of energy that acts as a transmitter of vibrations to an individual; sometimes seen connected to the physical and the soul body.

Skyclad. In the nude.

Soul Body. The spiritual counterpart of the physical body; the immortal part of an individual's personality that can travel independently and survives death.

Soul Guide. A spirit who guides an individual and assists in one's progress, development, and well-being.

Soul Travel. The spiritual art of traveling in the soul body.

Spirit Helper. A spirit who temporarily or periodically acts as a guide to further an individual's progress or well-being.

Succubus. A female entity from the lower astral realms that feeds off human energy (see Incubus).

Tantra. Umbrella term for Eastern spiritual discipline that uses sacred sexuality as a path to enlightenment.

Telepathy. Non-verbal communication using the exchange of thoughts.

Thought Form. An etheric manifestation resulting from positive or negative actions, thoughts, and emotions.

Trickster. A usually harmless but dramatic spirit or entity that changes form.

Tunnel. An etheric passageway that connects the physical world to the invisible planes; the passage a soul uses to enter various planes of existence beyond the physical world.

Vicarious Spirit. A spirit or entity who feeds off of human emotion, sexuality, or addiction; can have a negative influence over an individual.

Yoni. Tantric term for the vagina (see Lingam).

Bondi, Julia. *Lovelight: Unveiling the Mysteries of Sex and Romance.* New York: Pocket Books, 1989.

Cunningham, Scott. *Encyclopedia of Magical Herbs.* Saint Paul, MN: Llewellyn, 1988.

Goldberg, B.Z. *The Sacred Fire: The Story of Sex in Religion.* New York: University Books, 1958.

Grahn, Judy. *Another Mother Tongue: Gay Words, Gay Worlds.* Boston: Beacon Books, 1990.

Hamilton, Edith. *Mythology: Timeless Tales of Gods and Heroes.* New York: New American Library, 1969.

Kumar, Acharya Sushil. *Song of the Soul.* Blairstown, NJ: Siddachalam Publications, 1987.

Psychic Voyages (Mysteries of the Unknown Series). New York: Time-Life Books, 1987.

Rice, Edward. *Eastern Definitions.* New York: Doubleday and Co., 1978.

Starhawk. *The Spiral Dance.* San Francisco: Harper & Row, 1989.

Walker, Barabara G. *The Woman's Encyclopedia of Myths and Secrets.* San Francisco: Harper & Row, 1983.

Waldemar, Charles. *The Mystery of Sex.* New York: Lyle Stewart, Inc., 1960.

Index

Index

☽ REACH FOR THE MOON

Llewellyn publishes hundreds of books on your favorite subjects! To get these exciting books, including the ones on the following pages, check your local bookstore or order them directly from Llewellyn.

ORDER BY PHONE

- Call toll-free within the U.S. and Canada, 1-800-THE MOON
- In Minnesota, call (612) 291-1970
- We accept VISA, MasterCard, and American Express

ORDER BY MAIL

- Send the full price of your order (MN residents add 7% sales tax) in U.S. funds, plus postage & handling to:

    Llewellyn Worldwide
    P.O. Box 64383, Dept. K247-X
    St. Paul, MN 55164–0383, U.S.A.

POSTAGE & HANDLING

(For the U.S., Canada, and Mexico)

- $4.00 for orders $15.00 and under
- $5.00 for orders over $15.00
- No charge for orders over $100.00

We ship UPS in the continental United States. We ship standard mail to P.O. boxes. Orders shipped to Alaska, Hawaii, The Virgin Islands, and Puerto Rico are sent first-class mail. Orders shipped to Canada and Mexico are sent surface mail.

International orders: Airmail—add freight equal to price of each book to the total price of order, plus $5.00 for each non-book item (audio tapes, etc.).

Surface mail—Add $1.00 per item.

Allow 2 weeks for delivery on all orders.
Postage and handling rates subject to change.

DISCOUNTS

We offer a 20% discount to group leaders or agents. You must order a minimum of 5 copies of the same book to get our special quantity price.

FREE CATALOG

Get a free copy of our color catalog, *New Worlds of Mind and Spirit*. Subscribe for just $10.00 in the United States and Canada ($30.00 overseas, airmail). Many bookstores carry *New Worlds*—ask for it!

Visit our web site at www.llewellyn.com for more information.

Astral Travel for Beginners
Transcend Time and Space with Out-of-Body Experiences

Richard Webster

Astral projection, or the out-of-body travel, is a completely natural experience. You have already astral traveled thousands of times in your sleep, you just don't remember it when you wake up. Now, you can learn how to leave your body at will, be fully conscious of the experience, and remember it when you return.

The exercises in this book are carefully graded to take you step-by-step through an actual out-of-body experience. Once you have accomplished this, it becomes easier and easier to leave your body. That's why the emphasis in this book is on your first astral travel.

The ability to astral travel can change your life. You will have the freedom to go anywhere and do anything. You can explore new worlds, go back and forth through time, make new friends and even find a lover on the astral planes. Most importantly, you will find that you no longer fear death as you discover that you are indeed a spiritual being independent of your physical body.

By the time you have finished the exercises in this book you will be able to leave your body and explore the astral realms with confidence and total safety.

1-56718-796-X
256 pp., 5³⁄₁₆ x 8 $9.95

The Astral Projection Kit

Denning & Phillips

When you can perform astral projection, you temporarily break the bonds holding mind and body together so that you can travel through space and time ... obtain higher knowledge ... communicate with those on the astral planes ... and more! Here is a complete kit to aid you in successful and conscious astral travel! You receive a 90-minute cassette tape, the book *The Llewellyn Practical Guide to Astral Projection,* and a meditation card with instructions to serve as your doorway into the astral planes. Easy step-by-step exercises allow you to safely travel the astral plane to renew your physical and emotional health, mental powers, spiritual attainment, and activate the development of psychic faculties.

0-87542-199-7
Boxed set: 5¼ x 8, 252 pp. book; 90-minute audio tape;
meditation card with instructions $24.95

Perfect Love
Find Intimacy on the Astral Plane
(Formerly titled *Astral Love*)

D. J. Conway

Here is a clear and complete system for developing your ability to astral travel. *Perfect Love* takes you beyond the world of mortals into the greatest adventure you will ever know. Learn how to develop a lasting relationship with an astral lover who will offer you emotional support and even help you to find a physical partner who is right for you. Meld chakras with divine beings in the ultimate sexual encounter. Boost your self-esteem through the healing effects of a relationship with a higher-level astral being who really cares about you.

Forging a personal relationship on the astral plane will enhance your life, filling it with love, compassion, understanding, and positive energy. Astral sex can even help you establish a stronger connection with the Divine and open new avenues of magick. Even if you choose not to be sexually active on the astral planes, you can establish strong, warm friendships with high-level beings to enhance your magick and spiritual advancement.

1-56718-181-3
192 pp., 6 x 9, illus., softcover $12.95

To order, call 1-800-THE MOON
Prices subject to change without notice